Plant Spirit Gardener

by Alanna Moore

Alanna Moore is also the author of:
Backyard Poultry – Naturally, 1998, 3rd edition 2014
Stone Age Farming - 2001, 2nd ed. 2013
Divining Earth Spirit - 1994, 2nd ed. 2004
The Wisdom of Water - 2007
Sensitive Permaculture - 2009
Water Spirits of the World - 2008, 2nd ed. 2012
Touchstones for Today - 2013

PLANT SPIRIT GARDENER

ISBN –978-0-9757782-9-6

 Published by Python Press.
Australia and Ireland -
Fairyfield, Corlisheen,
Carrick on Shannon, Co Leitrim.
www.pythonpress.com
pythonpress@gmail.com

Text design, editing and typesetting also by Alanna Moore.
All photographs by Alanna Moore except the following. Photos on pages 20, 21, 66, 71, 109, 111, 115, 125, 127, 133, 134, 140, 147, 149, 163, plus one on the cover - by Peter Cowman. Photo page 12 by Sigrid Böhme. Photo page 150 by Kate Twomey.

Diagrams and illustrations by Alanna Moore, except for page 84, by Craig Thompson, and pages 26 and 36, from Dover Graphics.

Printed on acid free paper by Lightning Source Inc., a company committed to manufacturing books in a manner that both respects the environment and helps preserve the world's natural resources.

Cover Photos - Top: Alanna Moore with her cabbage Big Max.
Left: Oak tree struck by lightening in Germany. Right: Tree hugging is good
for you! Photo page 1: Earth spirit house at a Buddhist Centre in Taiwan.

Introduction

This book is an ode to trees and the spiritual dimensions of the plant kingdom. We need trees now more than ever, so I hope it gives extra impetus for planting them and that it enhances a sense of the sacred in gardeners and landcarers.

As well as ancient folklore and scientific insights, there are clairvoyant descriptions to illuminate the spiritual realities of Mother Nature. You can even use this book as a practical divining tool for learning to dowse (also called divining), experience other dimensional life and energetically enhance the environment. By following the suggested exercises and applying dowsing to the summaries, charts and lists provided, honing the intuitive faculties can be easy. You can become self-empowered to be a backyard shaman. And you too can grow great big cabbages!

With gratitude for their inspiration:

I must pay homage to the giants who have gone before me, lit the way and are now sadly deceased. Tree planting extraordinaires Richard St. Barbe-Baker and Western Australia's Barry Oldfield OA. Dowsers Esther Deans and Isabel Bellamy of Sydney. Geoffrey Hodson and Billy Arnold, both amazing seers of the other-dimensional worlds of nature. Bill Mollison, the permaculture pioneer I first met 30 years ago when he signed my copy of the 'Permaculture Designer's Manual' and wrote in it - *Great big cabbages to you!* His recent passing calls for all who knew him or was impressed by his works, to plant a tree in his memory. Hats off also to the late Prof. Phil Callahan for his brilliant insights, such as into the yin and yang of stone energies.

With gratitude for contributors to this book:

Peter Cowman (for technical help, photos and much encouragement), Martin Richter, Kate Twomey, Kate Wimble, Sigrid Böhme, David Kennet, Mike and Zhor Wust, Alice Khuan, Madis Senner, Renan Cengiz, Mique, Sharon Quigley, Michael Haxeltine, Ced Jackson, Stefanie Keitel, Peter Archer, Dr Hilary Bond, Dr Geo, Wojcech Pukarski.

Table of Contents

chakra dowsing 118, Plant spirit dowsing 120, Drawing up the sap 122, Indoor plant fairy 122, Dowsing sick trees 123, Energetic enhancement by visualisation 124.

Chapter seven: Dowsing in the garden   page 125

Chapter eight: Gardening with the devas   page 147

Chapter nine: Divine gardening   page 169

References
Resources

Diagrams

Chapter Summaries

Dowsing Charts and Lists

Chapter one:
What plants give us

Chapter one:
What plants give us

"Plants are important transformers of energy, stepping down the Sun's energy into a form of nourishment that we can use. The same is true on other levels; plants step down spiritual energies for our use. Without plants we could not maintain ourselves on any level." Peter Aziz

The benefits bestowed by plants

From earliest times across the world, plants have been central to the success of human societies. We owe so much to plants, from the lowliest algae, to the mightiest of trees. They generously provide a multitude of benefits from their fruit and nuts, wood, fibre, sap, leaves, bark, flowers, pollen, seeds and roots. Also from their subtle energies and intelligence.

We can breathe, thanks to the oxygen that plants produce. Plants remove carbon dioxide from the atmosphere and store it long term. They are a great boon for reversing climate change, as they benefit from increased levels of carbon dioxide in the atmosphere. This fertilising factor means that they are nowadays growing at much faster rates, thereby hastening its removal. Higher CO_2 levels also provide plants with increased protection against drought stress, because their leaves have smaller stomata, reducing moisture loss potential. So a hotter and drier greenhouse world can be a much greener one! [1]

Plants are co-creators of soil, their roots bringing up minerals from deep down to fertilise topsoil. Plants protect topsoil by holding it together with their roots and sheltering and feeding it with the mulch of their fallen leaves. Humus from the decomposing leaves builds up a mineral-rich colloidal insulating layer, greatly enriching soil and acting as an organic diffusion filter that separates the negatively charged ground from the positively charged atmosphere.

Plants generate rainfall through evapo-transpiration. Essential to healthy water catchments, the forest is the 'cradle of water', with incoming waters collected, filtered and purified in the water cycle. Plants also purify the atmosphere, absorbing some air pollution, as well as removing the hazard of electro-magnetic pollution to some degree.

Plants regulate temperature. They keep the land cool under their shade. This happens on a vast scale, with forests moderating global warming. Forests being important carbon sinks, they thus have significant stabilising effects on temperatures globally. [2] Vegetation also blocks the destructive force of the wind, thus reducing evaporation of soil moisture and wind-blown soil loss. When forests are removed, rainfall is reduced and topsoil erodes away, the land becomes dry and infertile.

Green environments have also nurtured the human soul for millennia. Our sacred relationships with plants have been the forerunner of many spiritual traditions. Trees have been held in special reverence and sacred lore proclaims them to be the wisdom keepers of the land. The world over, people have sought out venerable trees to pray and meditate beneath. To the Zoroastrians, this was the way to Heaven. [3]

Tree of Life

The *World Tree*, also known as the *Cosmic Tree* and *Tree of Life*, is a potent symbol of natural power found in diverse human cultures. Mediating between Heaven and Earth, in ancient Vedic descriptions from India the World Tree was the very body of Brahma, the god of creation, bearing the other deities on its branches. Later, early Buddhist literatured depicted the Buddha as a tree. In Europe the World Tree was the mighty Ash; in Russia - the equally mighty Oak.

In some cultures Cosmic Trees were associated with death as well as life. To the Egyptians, the Sycamore Fig and its goddess welcomed the souls of the dead to the afterlife, spraying its sap, the elixir of immortality, over them in tomb wall paintings. The Djed pillar, symbolising Egyptian god Osiris, was another vegetative cosmic axis, taking the form of a tree trunk with lopped limbs. [4]

In ancient shamanic rituals performed world-wide, the World Tree acted as a portal to the Upper-world and it would be ceremonially climbed. Re-creation and participation with such a local axis mundi occured in pre-Christian Europe. Here the village Maypole was, and still is, decorated and danced around in spring and summertime, in echoes of the celebration of an annual 'resurrection of the plant world'.

Left: A Maypole towers over the village of Akams, in Allgau, Bavaria.

Below: The annual Maypole dance, Mt Franklin, Victoria, Australia.

For the Navaho, and other nations in south western USA, the sacred axis of their world is a giant Corn plant (Zea mays). In their emergence myth, a *path of blessing* runs up this plant. This was ascended by mythical ancestor heroes, who went up it to the various Sky worlds for severe initiation ordeals by fire and water. A sand painting of this is created on the ground as part of a therapeutic ritual of 'returning to origins' through re-enactment. Healing effects are sought, with the patient often seated on the sacred image during the ritual. [4]

Sacred trees

Across the forested regions of the ancient world, sacred groves of trees served as leafy temples and places of sanctuary. Often these *nemetons* were located on hilltops or at points of strong Earth power. (Nemeton is their Celtic name, the Romans called them *luci*. [5]) Sometimes a tradition developed of erecting simple altars beneath the stately canopies, as a focus for people to express gratitude for nature's bounty, or for invoking nature's wisdom and goodwill.

In some cultures the first temples evolved from these altars and early temple complexes subsequently had sacred groves retained close by. The Acropolis in Athens, for example, has evidence of one. However in northern regions and westwards, Druid priests of the old religion needed no temples, but merely the green groves themselves. (The word Druid relates them to the Oak tree.) Anglo-Saxon and Norse peoples gathered under sacred groves for all matters of council, jurisdiction and regular seasonal celebrations. Their favourites were Yew and Linden.

Sacred tree traditions are found in ancient religious writings. Jewish tradition, following Canaanite fashion, was to worship God at tree sanctuaries. Moses was said to have a staff made from Almond wood, the sacred tree of Israel, its old Semitic name being Amygdala, or Great Mother. Jesus taught his followers in the sacred Olive grove of Gethsemane. On his last night, the Bible relates, Jesus went to this Olive grove and there met an angel who gave him strength.

Tree veneration in Europe was once widespread. Individual sacred trees were often retained in the Christian era and re-sanctified, with a Madonna statue placed in them. (The photo overleaf shows a sacred

11

Linden tree beside the main street in the village of Bad Kohlgrub in Bavaria.) But generally, the new religion saw a crusade against sacred trees that was widespread and relentless. Destroying them for purely religious reasons up until medieval times, with numerous papal edicts against them from the 5th century onwards, the practise escalated as the demand for construction timber rose. Five important sacred trees in Ireland, the axis mundis of their tribes, were all felled by the late 7th century. In the 11th century many German tribes still worshipped nature beneath their sacred trees in remote forests, but there are records of bishops ordering their destruction. Sacred groves lasted a bit longer in eastern Europe. In Lithuania they were not wiped out until the 14th century, however tree veneration continued quietly up until the 19th century.

Trees and serpents of knowledge

In legends, art and decorative motifs spanning the world, sacred trees of life and knowledge are often teamed up with the sacred serpent of wisdom. This was the case from ancient Sumeria to Scandinavia and up until the Biblical Garden of Eden, with its (demonised) serpent.

Overleaf: Tree & serpent on an Irish crest of bardic family the O'Duignans, and another on an old building facade in a Zurich city street.

In countries such as India, this tradition continues today. In Tamil Nadu, sacred tree shrines are commonly found on the outskirts of villages. These are visited by women desiring children. A stone image of the divine cobra or entwined cobra pair is placed beneath the tree, typically an aged Ashvatta, also known as a Pippal or Bodhi tree (Ficus

religiosa). This *nagakal* carving, representing the snake virgin Goddess Nakamal, is first submerged in a spring or pond for several months, to be impregnated with Earth energy.

The woman then goes to visit the tree shrine and ritually circumambulates it while saying prayers, up to one hundred and eight times. She then establishes her snake stone under the tree, or in the precincts of a temple, whereafter she regularly visits and ritually sprinkles it with turmeric and milk. [6]

Previous page: Tree shrine in a large temple complex in Kanchipur, Tamil Nadu, India.

Left: Nagakals and sacred tree at a Tamil Nadu roadside shrine.

Around the world, sacred trees continue to be venerated for sharing with us their powers of wisdom, vitality, healing and fertility. The more deeply they are valued, the less likely it is that communities will allow forests to be destroyed for monetary profit. No wonder the forces of capitalism aligned with mainstream religion to outlaw pagan sentiments. They were paving the way for wholesale plundering of Mother Earth.

Plant interactions

The powerful symbol of the *Tree of Knowledge* has been widespread since ancient times. It is not surprising then that the intelligence of plants has started to come to light in modern understanding. In terms of plants interacting intelligently between themselves, scientists have known for around thirty years that plants communicate together by releasing volatile chemicals into the atmosphere. This can happen with plants being attacked by pests. The chemical messages are picked up by neighbouring plants, who then prepare to defend themselves. The classic example is that of trees growing in stands on the African savannahs. When a herd of giraffes turn up and start nibbling Acacia trees, they react by secreting extra tannin and other unpalatable alkaloids into their vulnerable leaves. A warning message is sent out by the trees to the rest of the grove and soon the others follow suit, the giraffes stop eating and leave them alone.

Other types of chemicals emitted by plants are aimed at attracting certain insect predators that eat the pests that attack them and their neighbours. While self-protecting, plants also extend their influence, with cooperative behaviour. They are looking out for each other.

And now scientists have found, below the forest floor, a parallel communication system, working through mycelial (fungal) networks in the ground. The fuzzy white cobweb-like mycelial network, which can extend over large areas, unlocks nutrients in soil and makes them available to plants. Actually more closely related to animals than to plants, fungi are nature's greatest recyclers and they are crucial to the creation of soil.

As well, American mycologist and author Paul Stamets believes that the mycelial networks are "information sharing membranes…[they] are aware, react to change, and collectively have the long-term health of the host environment in mind". Highly responsive to changes in the environment and in constant dialogue with it, they respond to rainfall and register the movement of animals across them. They emit attractants such as sweet fragrances on the forest floor and scent trails.

Mycelial nets take the same archetypal form as neuronal networks in our brains, as well as the pattern of the internet, of hurricanes and probably vast structures in the universe, as envisioned in string theory. Stamets describes this "sentient membrane …[as the] neurological network of nature… Earth's natural internet, a consciousness with which we might be able to communicate". [7]

Mycorrhizal fungal networks are the type that specifically live and work with plants in mutually beneficial relationships. Most plants seem to have co-evolved with these fungi, who partner with the plant roots and, by their decomposing ability, make soil nutrients more easily absorbable for them. They also pass on to plants various chemicals that protect against disease and pestilence. In exchange, the fungi feed off sugars secreted from the plant roots. Mycorrhizal networks can connect individual trees in a forest together across, sometimes, vast areas.

More knowledge of plant interactions has come from recent experiments in Canada. These show that injury of a plant results in the transmission of alarm signals that spread through the underground 'internet' to neighbours. The receiving plants then respond, with increased defensive gene expression and enzyme activity, increased pest resistance and the like, reports Suzanne Simard, professor of forest ecology at the University of British Columbia.

"Trees share water, macronutrients, micronutrients, carbon, biochemical signals, allelochemicals or hormones from one plant to another, mostly for mutual benefit and protection," says Simard. An expert in this field, she finds that recognition of kin is also evident between established and regenerating trees that are linked into the mycelial network. Trees mostly shuttle micro-elements to close relatives. However large old *Mother Trees* also share small amounts of resources with strangers. [8]

These discoveries give humanity ample reason to retain and protect the mighty Grandparent Trees of the forest.

In Germany, which has about 30% forest coverage, forest ranger and author Peter Wohlleben has delighted readers with his descriptions of forest trees as being essentially social beings. In 'The Hidden Life of Trees' - the best selling German non-fiction book of 2015 - he tells how

trees can count, learn and remember; nurse sick neighbours; warn each other of danger by messaging across the 'Wood Wide Web'; and even keep the ancient stumps of long-felled companions alive for centuries by feeding them a sugar solution through the roots. [9]

And so the forest gives us a magnificent model of the deep interconnectedness of lifeforms and of a caring society based on co-operative behaviour.

We have much to learn from the plant kingdom!

Australian Aboriginal Tree Telephones
by Sharon Quigley, Perth, Australia.

"In Western Australia the Aboriginal people in the bush use the trees to communicate messages to each other. Over the years I have been told this several times, by different friends plus Aboriginal students of mine.

"For the Aboriginal people, the trees are their spiritual telephone system! They speak to the trees and tell the trees their message and who the message is for and the trees pass the message from tree to tree along the way, until the message gets to the intended person.

"This is used in everyday life, for example something as simple as the men out hunting, telling their women who are miles away that they are heading home with food, so the women can get the fire ready for cooking and it will be ready when the men arrive back at camp, which could be at any time of the day!"

Aboriginal Birthing Trees

Traditions of healing trees are found globally. For example, women once resorted to certain trees to give birth beneath, receiving spiritual strength and support, as well as pain relief from them. The author remembers the *Birthing Tree* at the La Perouse Aboriginal Reserve, in Sydney, Australia, on the shores of Botany Bay. Many of the local Aboriginals there are direct descendants of those met by Captain Cook in 1770, prior to the white invasion.

This particular Birthing Tree was an exotic species, a large specimen of Indian Coral beneath which many of the older residents had been born. For a few years during childhood in the 1960's my family lived across the road from it. Returning years later, we celebrated the Birthing Tree with local school children at a wonderful event held in the early 1980's, when the author was running the group Children of the Green Earth, an offshoot of Men of the Trees.

Plants and our health

Plants are not only an essential source of oxygen, they also emit human health-promoting negative ions. (They do this when transpiring water vapour.) Plants can absorb air pollution and so help to improve air quality both indoors and out. The moist atmosphere around them is a delight to breathe. And there is plenty of other evidence that interacting with plants is excellent for the health and spirit of humankind.

Studies show that people recover faster from surgery and take fewer drugs if their hospital room has a view of greenery. Other research finds that mothers with more trees around their homes are less likely to have underweight babies. People placed in a natural environment have reduced blood pressure, improved heart rate and other stress indicators, other studies have found.

On the other hand, tree loss can have negative outcomes for public health. One example, from a survey of 1,300 American counties where Emerald Ash borer was destroying forests, showed that where trees had declined, the human mortality rate (specifically from lower respiratory tract and cardiovascular illnesses) was significantly elevated.

Benefits gained from visiting green places and tree hugging are described in Matthew Silverstone's 2011 book 'Blinded by Science'. They are a result, he says, of trees having "unique vibrational patterns which cause positive changes in our biological behaviours when touched". Beneficial effects include helping with mental illnesses, Attention Deficit Hyperactivity Disorder (ADHD), concentration levels, depression and headaches.

One study cited showed that being in green places "may be as effective as prescription drugs in treating some forms of mental illnesses".

Children especially can gain extreme psychological and physiological benefits of improved health and well-being from interacting with plants. When kids are in green areas they function better cognitively and emotionally, and enjoy more creative play. Students with pot plants in their classrooms have been found to perform better in examinations. [10]

Dowsers have been using their own methods to determine the benefits of plant contact. The author uses pendulum dowsing to assess energetic effects. Dowsing has shown that people's auras will expand to double in size after just two minutes of hugging a tree, which, of course, can feel wonderfully revitalising! When the Devon Dowsers group in the UK did their own study, spokesman Tony Heath reported that:

"We noted a general uplift in our energy levels whilst tree hugging". [11]

Forest Therapy

Some of the benefits of going for a walk in a forest come as a result of breathing in health-promoting vapours that are emitted by trees. Evergreens, in particular, are noted for their aromatic chemical emissions, called *phytoncides*, that help to open up airways, reduce stress hormones, increase cerebral blood flow and boost the immune system. In Japan, which has a whopping 64% forest cover, the Forestry Agency in 1982 started to promote visits to forests for health purposes. This *Shinrin-Yoku* (Forest Bathing or Basking) became very popular with people and it went on to become a recognised relaxation and stress management activity in Japan.

But in most other countries, people in the urban world are often severely disconnected from nature. *Nature Deficit Syndrome* is the label given to this condition. Now a new modality has been developed to cure the problem - *Forest Ecotherapy*. Studies show the valuable physical, psychological and social health benefits of Forest Ecotherapy, which is also known as Forest Therapy in the USA.

Ireland's first professional Forest Therapist Shirley Gleeson explained what a typical eco-therapeutic forest walk would entail.

"People are encouraged to use their five senses through sensory connection invitations and mindfulness activities in a forest setting. A typical walk lasts about three hours and people are introduced to the wonders, beauty and peace of the forest ecosystem. The pace is very gentle, which encourages people to slow down and come out of their heads and into their bodies.

"The sense of interconnectedness that people experience can be spiritual in nature. After these walks, people describe having more energy, being more relaxed and seeing the forest with new eyes," she said. [12]

Chapter two:
Plant spirits

Chapter two:
Plant spirits

"Nearly all well-grown trees have attached to them, in addition to innumerable nature spirit builders, an advanced nature spirit or a God."
Geoffrey Hodson

Who are the plant spirits?

Since ancient times, the perception that landscapes are inhabited by intelligent nature beings of other-dimensional worlds has been universally recognised. Sanskrit gives these beings a generic name of *devas*, meaning 'the shining ones'. While psychologists might explain deva legends as a mythical playing out of human archetypes, their spiritual actuality is also obvious to indigenous peoples of the world.

Animists have traditions of the many 'species' of devic life, while modern clairvoyants describe the changing variety of plant spirits associated with plants. A deva is firmly attached to the life of each individual plant, while overlighting devas preside over a particular species. Tiny devas work with flowers, leaves or fruit only. More highly evolved devas care for all the various plants in their territory, so each garden might have it's own chief garden fairy. In cold regions during winter, many devas are dormant and hibernating, waiting for the call to action in springtime.

Plant spirits have features in common with humans, in that they are composed of much the same type of subtle energies. Clairvoyant vision describes their basic form as balls of energy, or points of light. Their spherical, inter-penetrating energy fields have several frequencies. In the case of larger, more highly evolved nature beings, *astral* matter comprises their larger field, a function of which allows them to resonate with and feel out their environment. (Astral being one of the many terms coined by the Theosophical movement that brought ancient Indian thought to the West over 130 years ago.) In humans the astral field is a vehicle for people's emotional life and nature beings can have strong emotional responses too.

The larger devas typically have a second, smaller and denser field of *etheric* matter, that provides a blueprint for their species' characteristics. They can also condense this field at will into different shapes, sizes or forms. The more highly evolved species can shape shift into recognisable characters from folkloric traditions. Or they may choose to take on the guise of a plant or animal that they admire. But they don't usually hold these visual forms for long, only when people are observing them and when they wish to be seen by them.

The role of the devas in nature is to stimulate the life of plants and help to guide their evolution. They feed off energy and reproduce by 'sub-dividing', popping out a little fractal/clone occasionally. In gardens there are likely to be several species resident, involved with diverse activities. Describing their everyday work, eminent clairvoyant Geoffrey Hodson observed tiny beings hovering around plants, appearing as energetic points of light. They were busy performing specific jobs of caring for their charges, expressing keen affection for them all the while. He saw them absorb energy from the atmosphere, then enter into the plant under their care, where they discharged the energy for the plant's benefit. When a new growth phase was imminent and new devas were called for, Hodson would hear certain sounds going out to attract them. [1]

"In the heart of every seed," he explained, "is a living centre, which contains the stored-up results of previous seasons as a vibratory possibility. Apparently the awakening, or stirring of the life in due season produces sound. This sound is heard throughout the elemental regions where the builders answer the call to labour. Every type of growth, whether of stem, shoot, leaf or flower appears to have its own note, or call, to which the appropriate nature spirit 'builder' must respond. This sound also has a form producing activity and is, probably, the means by which the archetypal form is translated to the etheric level."

"In the early stages, when only the green shoot is appearing," he went on, "the builders of a certain order are employed; tiny etheric creatures, appearing as points of light... When the flower-stem and flower are to be built, a new set of builders arrives on the scene. Apparently these are more advanced, for, on their arrival, the whole process of growth is quickened and stimulated...and, as soon as colouration is to begin, the fairies proper appear and implant their special rate of vibration." These stay around until the work of the builders is complete, taking great pleasure and pride in 'their' plant. "When the completely flowered condition is reached, the full chord is sounding forth," said Hodson, who sometimes perceived this ethereal chord as a scent.

The incessant activity of plant devas has also been described by clairvoyant observer Dora van Gelder, who tells of how plant fairies help plants to manage their energetic uptakes, from the sun in particular. Normally doing this outdoors, she has seen some species even caring for plants inside hot houses. Common garden species she described as being butterfly or candle-like in appearance. But the typical garden fairy, that would be the stuff of 'fairy tales', is bigger, at around 500 mm - 600 mm tall, and has more intelligence plus a more human-like appearance, she says. (But not much like a typical illustration, such as on the right.) These fairies work at supervising the activities of lesser devas in the garden, amongst other jobs, with their primary nourishment  derived from the sun's energy. Dawn is when their work begins, starting with a group celebration. Van Gelder took great delight in watching fairies hover around their favourite plants, checking that all is well with them and pouring out their love and joy in the process. [2]

Mannikins are small (a few inches/centimetres tall) nature beings with a man-like appearance that are associated with most types of vegetation, and, according to Hodson, they are "the most common fairy type" in England. He observed them living within tree trunks and branches, their work being connected with the growth and colouration of branches and leaves. Autumn is a very busy time for them. Mannikins also derive energetic nourishment from the tree and Hodson saw one tired looking mannikin going inside it's tree's trunk, only to reappear ten minutes later all lively and rejuvenated. [1]

Corn gods

In agricultural areas of the world, *corn gods* evolved with human society in the birth of early religions, *corn* being an old English term originally used for all grain crops. The annual birth/germination, growth, then death/harvesting of the gods and their crops provided cycles of certainty for early societies, and the basis for seasonal celebrations. In south-west America, for example, the Pawnee nation's creation myth of their emergence from the Underworld, has Mother Corn leading the people to the surface, with a cry of *All is completed! All is perfect!* [3]

In Greek myth, Demeter ('Great Mother') resided on Mount Olympus as one of twelve chief gods. Ever-youthful, the immortal gods dined on Ambrosia, a honey infused with multiple flower essences. Demeter's main symbols were a sickle and an ear of Wheat or Barley; she may also be depicted holding a burning torch, or wearing a crown and sceptre. Her gift to mankind was the knowledge of cereal cultivation. Demeter's other sacred plant was the Poppy, a weed of Barley fields, and her sacramental drink must have been some sort of beer. Her animal was the serpent, a pair of which was harnessed up to convey her chariot around. Ceres is her Roman equivalent, as was Ceridwen for Celtic tribes.

Demeter partnered with chief god Zeus and bore him a daughter, called Kore in childhood. When a maiden, Kore was picking flowers one day. Suddenly the Earth opened up and Hades, chief god of the Underworld, popped up and whisked her away. Demeter's grieving for her lost daughter caused the land's fertility to wither. Leaves fell from trees and nothing grew. Now called Persephone (a name meaning 'she who brings destruction'), as the mature Queen of the Underworld, she eventually returned to live with her mother for the rest of the year. Then, fertility was at last restored and springtime initiated. Her annual return to Hades signalled winter's onset. Thus the changing seasons were explained. [4]

There is another ancient vegetation myth from Mespotamia. Chief goddess Innana, also known as Ishtar, travelled down to the Underworld, while the Earth above grew sterile. She confronted her sister, Ereskigal the ruler of the Underworld, and was killed there. But she was revived and returned home. The deal for Innana to stay there was that her husband, vegetation god Dumuzi, must spend each winter in the Underworld. When he returns to her each year, springtime commences.

Similar themes are found associated with sun and corn goddess Aine of Irish legend. In an ancient ritual of possible Mediterranean or Middle Eastern origins, farmers waved flaming torches around the corn fields at midnight of mid-summer's day, to stimulate the growing crops. Emulating their chief goddess, this tradition was kept up until recent times on Aine's sacred hill, Knockaine in County Limerick, in the fertile fields of one of the first areas where wheat growing was introduced.

Crom Dubh, Aine's partner, was the most important of the Irish gods, popular mainly in the north and western seaboard, from Donegal Bay down to the Dingle Peninsula. Said to be dark skinned, this god of harvest, the 'dark, stooped one', as his name translates, was regarded as the bringer of wheat and knowledge of its cultivation to Ireland. Middle Eastern origins of the Irish may explain Crom's dark skin. Geneticists working with archaeologists have reported DNA evidence of massive migration to Ireland from there thousands of years ago (Irish Times, 28/12/2015). "Sequencing the genome of an early woman farmer, who lived near Belfast 5,200 years ago, showed her majority ancestry originated in the Middle East, where agriculture was invented," they said. The woman farmer had black hair and brown eyes. Other Irish genomes from 4,000 years ago were found to have originated from the Pontic steppe on the shores of the Black Sea.

Now almost completely forgotten in Ireland, Crom Dubh appears to have reigned in the Underworld during winter, coming up to preside, alongside Aine, over the growing of the corn in summer. He was also associated with bulls and hilltops. Crom is best remembered at the 2,500BCE Grange stone circle beside Lough Gur in Limerick, in a story with classic corn myth elements. At the traditional start of harvest on August 1st (Lughnasa) each year, Crom claimed the *first fruits*, in the form of Eithne the corn maiden. Carrying this first sheath of corn on his back (hence his stoop) from Aine's birthing chair, a stone on the lake

Right: Crom's only image, at Cloghane, County Kerry, is reminiscent of Polynesian godstones, placed in gardens for watching over crops.

shore, he then proceeded to the nearby Grange stone circle. Entering the embanked stone circle, the largest of its kind in Ireland, he followed it's stone pathway - aligned to the August 1st sunrise. Crom finally stopped at the biggest megalith and there descended down into the Underworld. A ritual commemoration of this was held annually on Crom's harvest feast day, locally called Black Stoop Sunday. Still today coins are left by Crom's stone, as in the photo below.

Irish farmers also once carried corn sheaths about on their backs, before donkeys became available and, for the poorest of them, until not that long ago. Another deity with a stoop is Kokopelli, south-west American god of agriculture, who is depicted loaded with embryonic babies on his back. Kokopelli plays a flute, making the connection between music, joy and agriculture.

Re-enactment of the ritual 'sacrifice' of the corn maiden was done to ensure continuing bounty of the Earth in which the seeds germinate. That Crom Dubh carries and lovingly places the corn seed into the womb of the Earth each year at the beginning of autumn is a practical image. This was originally the time when farmers would, after harvest, sow the next year's crop. (And in this light, the so-called 'rape' of Persephone was probably just a misinterpretation of classic mysteries of the agricultural cycle, that were personified by the life phases of the triple corn goddess.)

Corn maiden Eithne, whose name means kernel or grain, was known in Ulster as Annie. Eithne is depicted in corn dollies and in the astrological sign for Virgo. Corn dollies woven from barley, wheat and oats evoke glyphs of this sun, cereal and fertility cult, which developed in Ireland from some 7,000 years ago. They are still being made, as you can see in the photo above of an Irish craft market stall.

Mairie MacNeill, who reviewed a mass of folklore about Irish harvest festivals, concluded that Crom is "a version of Donn" (a very early god, whose name means Dark or Brown), and that also "he can be regarded as identical with the pre-Celtic food-providing gods Cormac, the Dagda, Elcmar, Midir and Balor". Crom, a god borne from the beginnings of Neolithic agriculture, sustained his people through to the modern era wielding the mighty Rannach, the staff of life. He even survived the onslaught of Christianity, but only just. The dark earthiness of this Underworld god was demonised by the church. Well, eventually this was the case. At first Crom's redeeming features were actually praised by St Patrick! In some early Christian stories he was even referred to as a 'generous landlord' and was taken on as St Patrick's helper. [5]

Left: Corn goddess & cornucopia, British Museum.

Mediterranean mythology has several male gods of the corn and other crops. In Greece, Underworld god Ploutos, Demeter's son, was a god of agricultural wealth. Demeter bore him after lying with the hero Iasion in a thrice-ploughed field. Zeus blinded him so that he would distribute wealth to all, without regard to merit.

Ploutus was often depicted as a boy holding a *cornucopia* (a horn overflowing with the fruits of the Earth) alongside Demeter. At first only associated with grain harvests, later he came to represent wealth in general terms. Some sculptures show him as an infant in the arms of Eirene, the goddess of peace, or Tykhe, goddess of fortune. In the theology of the Eleusian Mysteries he was the Divine Child. Ploutos was identified with Plouton, the god Hades in his role as deity of Earth's hidden stores of wealth. [6]

In a Greek cult from the 6th century BCE, Dionysus, a late comer to Olympus, was originally a god of nature, woodlands, fertility and vegetation. Later he became more associated with wine, poetry and music, and was depicted with a wine cup and a wand. Dionysus convenes over the joyful relationship between man and nature, he was associated with annual carnivals and the origins of theatre. The Romans called him Bacchus. By the 5th century BCE his cult was widespread throughout Greece, however he was originally the Anatolian god of Lydia and Phrygia, in modern-day Turkey. Viniculture is still practised there. [7] The grape vine was also sacred to Egyptian god Osiris.

In South America, the cultivation of staple crop Sweet Potato also involved mythic traditions. There, fertility goddess Pachamama presides over planting and harvesting, the Andes mountains and earthquakes. Her shrines are special rocks, or the boles of legendary trees. She is pictured bearing harvests of potatoes and coca leaves.

Sweet Potatos spread from South America into the vast Pacific basin and planting traditions followed the crop. According to New Zealand Maori tradition, agriculture god Rongo partnered with goddess Te Pani. Their union made the Peace Child, the Kumara, or Sweet Potato.

Traditional farmers of the region know well how to keep their gods happy and gardens growing - they refrain from bad thoughts or feelings while gardening, so as not to upset the Peace Child. [8]

Plant totems

Ancient religions often gave agricultural produce a totemic status, where people enacted rituals of intense identification with the crop. Echoes of this continue today, such as in the Eucharist ritual in Catholicism, where the 'blessed sacrament', a wafer of Wheat, is celebrated as representing the 'real presence' of the body of Christ. The Eucharist ritual was suppressed in the Protestant church at the time of the Reformation, no doubt for being too pagan.

The concept was probably borrowed from earlier traditions of vegetation gods. For example, Demeter's annual mystery celebrations in Eleusis involved the displaying, in great solemnity before the gathered pilgrims, of a stalk of the sacred Wheat, no doubt grown in the temple grounds.

For Hopi people in the USA, Mother Earth is personified by the Corn Mother and they say that the corn itself (in this case - Maize, Zea mays) is "a living entity with a body similar to man's in many respects, and the people build its flesh into their own." Thus the sacrificed Maize spirit is continually resurrected by man's growing and eating of it, across the ever-sustaining cycles of life. [3]

In ancient Egypt the Festival of Ploughing began with the goddess Isis in her shrine "stripped naked and a paste made from the grain placed in her bed and moistened with water, representing the fecund earth". This sacred Egyptian ritual was "climaxed by the eating of the sacramental god, the Eucharist by which the celebrants were transformed, in their persuasion, into replicas of their god-man". [9]

Totemic plant associations go back much further in time than this and were important aspects of hunter-gatherer beliefs also. In Australian Aboriginal tradition, which goes back around 50,000 years, ancestral beings in the Dreamtime, taking both human and food plant or animal and other forms, were responsible for creating landscape features and laying down the laws of human behaviour, including food collection.

At birth, a particular animal or plant totem would be bestowed on an individual in a moiety group of a clan. Traditionally one's totem plant or animal was never killed out of respect, or a ceremony was conducted to appease the totem, if it was allowed to be eaten. Related people of other moieties and totems would be allowed to eat that plant or animal. Thus the environment and it's flora and fauna were maintained on a sustainable and biodiverse basis. These traditions continue today.

Totemic beings (fractals, or clones of deva species) are attached to their people's auras for life. Other totems can be acquired at later times and an individual can have several. The traditional rules of marriage insist on the correct relationship of moiety groupings. So totems also foster peaceful relations between different groups and human genetic diversity, as well as imparting spiritual benefits to people.

Clairvoyant researcher Billy Arnold described seeing totemic beings at Alice Springs in the year 2000. A huge mob of Aboriginal people had come from far and wide to see the Olympic torch being carried through town, as part of the lead-up to Sydney's Olympic Games. In a film about his work made by the author ('Pilgrimage to Central Australia') Billy recalled the amazing sight, from a spiritual perspective, at Emily Gap.

The scene was crowded with nature spirits that came along with the people. Seeing the powerful spirits travelling with them, Billy felt that they must be the peoples' totems. He was so blown away by the sight that tears were rolling down his cheeks when some children asked him if he was ok. He told them what he was seeing and asked them if he was correct in his understanding, that they must be the peoples' totems.

"Yeh, we know about those totem spirits.
That is what you are seeing!" they said to him.

Tree gods

Since time immemorial, trees have been revered as sacred holders of wisdom and healing for mankind, as well as divine guardians of the land. Important events were once held beneath sacred trees and they were thought to observe and record such events, and to make these memories available for people who might later tap into them.

In South Australia, for example, Urumbulla was a significant storyline (also known as a songline) for the Nukunu Aboriginal people. Urumbulla is one of the longest storylines in the country, running from Port Augusta on the south coast right up through to the Cape of Carpentaria in the far north. "Prior to the hospital being built at Port Augusta, there was a very large tree there and this tree actually captured some of the main stories," said Michael Turner, chairman of the Nukunu nation. Spirits associated with this tree were protectors of the Seven Sisters (Pleiadies constellation), Umawara Lake and the local region. [10]

In Europe certain large trees and their individual spirits, known as *dryads* or *fauns*, were consulted for their great sagacity and even became renowned as oracles. The prophetic Oak at Greece's Sacred Grove of Dodona, in the 'land of the Oak trees', near Greece's northern border with Albania, is a good example. Here pilgrims converged for over 2,000 years, up until the 4th century BCE. The sounds of rustling Oak leaves and the gushing of spring water from the Oak tree's base were interpreted by priestesses who were consulted for sometimes critical matters of state.

Right: The UK's famous
White Leaved Oak tree.

Many deities seem to have evolved from human veneration of important tree spirits. The Oak god Zeus is a good example. Zeus was reared in a cave in a forest. He was typically depicted as a strong, mature man with thick hair crowned with an Oak leaf wreath and a stern, bearded face, seated on a throne with his eagle, a wand in one hand and thunderbolt in the other. Dodona was his oracle centre. Zeus eventually became chief god, presiding over all the other gods on Mount Olympus, that towers nearly 3,000 metres high in the north of Greece. [7]

Oak trees have been sacred to other chief gods around the northern hemisphere too. These include Yahweh/Jehovah, Roman Jupiter and Juno, the Dagda in Ireland, Thor, Donar, Allah, Taranis and Perkunas in Scandinavia. Hercules (Heracles) famously wielded an Oak club. [11] Russian mythology has the World Tree as an Oak growing on a hilltop along with thunder god Perun and, at its base, serpent god Volos under a stone. The Russian Oak tree spirit itself is known as Dubynia and he is portrayed as a strong man carrying a club.

The association of Oaks with thunder and lightning is common and for good reason. Known to 'court the flash', this deep rooted tree loves to grow over underground water and often also grows in isolated positions, making it highly vulnerable. Indeed, Oaks are more likely to be struck by lightning than most other trees. Lightning strikes cause much damage and often trees regrow in a 'stag headed' shape, making them appear all the more divine!

Sculpture by Norman Lindsay, Blue Mountains, NSW, Australia

Overleaf: Lightning-struck Oak tree, Rheinberg, Germany (see also page 87) and Celtic forest deity Cernunnos.

Pan, the Greek pre-Olympian *Horned God* of the wild mountains of Arcadia, was a ruler of forests and animals, a protector of flocks and shepherds. Normally sporting stag's horns and good humoured, he could change suddenly, giving animals and people a fright and causing *panic*, literally! In Italy his equivalent,

Faunus, was another ancient rural deity, a bestower of fruitfulness on woods, fields and flocks. Faunus eventually became primarily a woodland deity, the sounds of the forest being regarded as his voice. As a god of prophecy, under the name of Fatuus, he was invoked at oracles in groves and wells.[12] Sylvanus is another Roman rural deity who presided over woods, fields, livestock and field boundaries. Fond of music, the pan pipes were sacred to him and he would be worshipped simply at a sacred grove or tree. Temples were not for him!

Cernunnos is the top Celtic *Lord of the Forest* and an equivalent of Pan. Depictions from many parts of western Europe often portray him with a beard, shaggy hair and antlers on his head. An image of a Cernunnos type figure found in Lombardy has been dated to the fourth millenium BCE. Around Berkshire, UK, legendary forest spirit Herne the Hunter is said to wear the antlers of a great stag. He was associated with a venerable Oak tree and Wild Hunts in the Windsor Forest.

When autumn comes, stags lose their antlers and vegetation goes dormant, the Horned Gods are also said to go into hibernation. Some legends locate them wintering in the Underworld. And when springtime comes, they return anew, sporting fresh horn buds that will grow into another pair of antlers over the summer.

The Green Man

Across Europe, we can see echoes of the Lord of the Forest. Intriguing masculine *Green Man* faces have been a feature of buildings from the Middle Ages onwards. With vegetation often lavishly streaming from their mouths,

Above: Green Man on a building in Zurich, Switzerland.

these faces and figures staring down from walls and ceilings at us evoke an 'Arcadian paradise' of the past. They recall the spirit of times past when mankind enjoyed greater resonance with nature. A token of respect for the old pagan paradigms perhaps?

The figures, first seen in the UK on ceilings in Manchester Cathedral from 1340, are typically faces composed mainly of Oak leaves with the odd acorn. Later flowers and fruit were included. Then, in a revival of Italian Renaissance building styles in the 19th century, they returned and the author has seen some charming examples on building facades in New Zealand, with many in Dunedin. [13]

The Green Man is no doubt also related to leafy figures in rural Britain representing Jack in the Green, the Wild Man, the May King and Robin Goodfellow (Robin Hood). People dressed as these festive characters would dance upon village greens in celebration of spring and the cycles of fertility and plenty. They represented ancient protectors of woods and wild places, from traditions of the arboreal cultures of their ancestors. Foliated heads were also a feature of classical Roman architecture around 2,000 years ago. Older examples are seen in mosaics from North Africa and similar figures have been found in India from 2,300 years ago. Green Men type faces have also been depicted in ancient China and Mexico. And to this day, in San Pablito, Puebla, Mexico, bark cutouts of people sprouting foliage are paraded during crop fertility rituals.

Rowan tree

Tree traditions in Europe

It was once a belief in Celtic Europe that the first people were born from trees, the first woman originally being a Rowan and the first man an Alder. On death, people were placed in hollowed out trees, then later in wooden coffins - taking them back to their origins.

Great intrinsic value was once placed on trees, as a reflection of the important economic and cultural values they held. Sanctuary was once granted by law to those sheltering beneath sacred trees in Ireland, where removing or injuring any tree under ancient Brehon (also Welsh) laws carried a range of stiff penalties associated with the value of each species. To cut down a sacred tree was absolutely taboo.

The ancient Irish royal centres were distinguished by grand specimens of sacred *Monument Trees*, also called *Trees of Power* or *Victory*, treasured as living symbols of the clan and the axis mundi of its sovereign power. During episodes of warfare these sacred trees were often targeted by rival tribes for extermination. They must have been quickly replaced, as there are records in the Irish Annals of sacred trees at particular locations being destroyed on subsequent occasions. Eventually there were a mere five sacred trees associated with Irish royal centres left, of such fame that they were celebrated in poetry. These are now long gone. Remarkably, the Brian Boru Oak, associated with one of Ireland's greatest kings, lives on. Some 1,000 years of age, it can be visited there, on the edge of the Woods of Raheen in County Clare.

Groves of trees have been the primordial temples for nature worship since earliest times. In Bath, UK, people once worshipped Nemetona, goddess of the sacred grove there. As well, the most important ceremonies and judicial proceedings were conducted under sacred trees and groves.

Tree shaped columns in temple and church architecture seem to be harking back to the sacred groves of old. An example, pictured right, is in the ancient temple of Hagia Sophia, Istanbul, Turkey.

On an everyday level of popular lore, there are many examples of pre-Christian veneration of trees in Europe surviving, fragmentally at least, in folktales and practises. Europe has a treasure trove of tree traditions and they are very similar in describing the spiritual attributes of each species. In

Ireland there was even an encoded system of writing, the Ogham alphabet, that references the lore of the sacred trees.

In Sweden, up until the 19th century, Lime, Ash or Elm were planted by country folk to act as guardian trees of the farmstead. The Ash Woman (Askafroa) deva was honoured with offerings of milk or beer. Norse mythology says that man was made from the Ash tree (Fraxinus excelsior) and woman from Elm (Ulmus procera and U. glabra), while Yggdrasil, the World Tree was first regarded as a Yew, then later as an Ash. Not surprisingly, the favourite weapons of the ancient past were originally spears made from Yew wood and later these were superseded by spears of Ash.

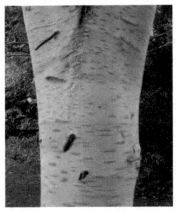

The protective spirit of Birch (Betula pendula and B. pubescens) was invoked when its wood was used for babies cradles and its twigs for brooms that are known as *besoms*. Around the time of the winter solstice, a besom was used to ritually sweep out from the home the old energies, to make way for the new year. After this, it was hung from the roof apex or above doorways.

Left: Birch tree trunk.

Rods of Birch were used in annual ritual perambulations of tribal boundaries, such as the 'Beating of the Bounds' in Britain. May Day fertility rites often took place in Birch groves until the medieval church put a stop to it. But the people then began to bring Birch trees into their villages and thus the Maypole and its associated festivities were spawned. In Siberia Birch is honoured as the World Tree, a 'deity of the door' guarding the way to the spirit world.

The Rowan (Sorbus aucuparia) has also been highly venerated as a household protector. Twigs of Rowan were placed above doorways to guard against misfortune, while its berries were worn to keep women safe. *Life Rods* of Rowan twigs were once used to ceremonially beat life into people, animals and fruit trees each spring. Like many trees associated with abundant life, Rowan was also sometimes associated with death and after-life. Druids planted it at sacred sites and invoked spirits by burning its wood. Aspen (Populus tremula) was originally regarded as an oracle, with messages divined from the sounds of its whispering leaves. It's associations with Druidry caused many trees to be axed in Christian times and it gained a reputation as being 'unlucky'.

Elm trees (Ulmus procera and U. glabra) were once esteemed as mediums between life and death, humans and devas. They were called Elven in England and Elfenholz (elfin wood) in Germany. Similarly, the magical Apple tree can link us to the Otherworlds, while an Apple gift symbolises love and abundance. An Apple tree features in the Biblical story of Adam and Eve eating it's forbidden fruit in the Garden of Eden.

A tradition from Apple growing areas of England, particularly in the south west, was to gather around the trees of the Apple orchard between mid-winter and new year for a session of *wassailing* (pronounced 'woss-olling'). Cider was drunk and offered to trees, along with cakes, and songs sung to encourage fruitfulness in the following year, to toast and thank the sacred Apple trees for the bounty to come.

The Oak (Quercus species) has deservedly been regarded as the king of trees, providing so many benefits from it's wood, tannin and medicine from the bark, plus acorns that were important as pig food. Huge old sacred Oaks were once considered places of sanctuary and people gathered beneath them for oath-taking and other ceremonies. Their memories live on in Britain, where we find *Gospel Oaks*, *Honour Oaks*, and *Royal Oaks* in locality names. Beneath *Marriage Oaks* it was fortuitous to be married. Oak is also considered to be a doorway between the worlds and it was commonly used to make strong front doors. Indeed the Irish Ogham letter Duir for Oak is also the word for door.

Hazel (Coryllus avellana) is a small tree associated with fertility and a dispenser of the sacred nuts of wisdom. To the ancient Irish it was a veritable Tree of Knowledge, source of pliable rods for divining and to make Druidic Life Rods from. In Greek and Roman myth, Hermes carries a caduceus staff made of a Hazel rod entwined by two snakes, as a symbol of wisdom and the healing arts. The medicine industry today continues to use this symbol.

Elder trees (Sambucus nigra, seen on the right) belong to the Great Goddess of northern Europe, Frau Holla of German fairy lore. Elder was the guardian of the farmyard and the Swedes gave her offerings of milk, the Prussians gave bread and beer, while the Scots put out milk and cakes for her. She was also seen as a guardian at the threshold to the Underworld. For Danes, the  Elder Mother protected households from bad luck, illness or evil spells. She could also convey fairy sight, while fairies were said to delight in playing in her branches. Before taking any of her wood, Elder was always asked most reverently and she was never totally cut down. Without permission granted, any resulting furniture made from Elder would be expected to be haunted. *Hats off to the Elder!* was an old Swiss and German saying.

Pine trees (Pinus species) have long been venerated too. Being evergreen, they were seen as holding everlasting power, while they also provided important sources of essential oils for cleansing, timber, fuel and waterproofing pitch. Just walking through a conifer wood has a toning, healing effect on the lungs. The bright light emitted from burning Pine was considered to be another of its cleansing powers. In Greek and Roman mythos the Pine was sacred to, amongst others, Pan.

Larch (Larix deciduas), a deciduous member of the conifer family, is a denizen of high mountains areas. In alpine traditions Larch is the home of the 'Blessed Ones', graceful, elf-like beings who are kind to people and animals. In other alpine parts the 'Blessed Maidens', dressed in white or silver and often perceived to be singing sweetly, are associated with Larch trees.

The Yew (Taxus baccata) is perhaps the most sacred of all the European trees. Capable of enormous lifespan, of over 4,000 years, this evergreen tree represents eternity and great wisdom. Its wood was made into weapons and wands and, in Nordic myth, Yew was the original World Tree itself. In Ireland's Munster province, the ruling Eoghanachta family and their goddess Danu were associated with Yew trees, the Eo being Yew. Many Celtic tribes were named after the Yew (the Eburones, Eburovices, Eburobriga, Eburmagus and Eburodunum).

Totally toxic, except for the red aril around the fruit, its wood was favoured for making spears and bows and today old specimens are generally only found in graveyards as a result. Which is not surprising because Yews are connected with the cult of the dead, the crone goddess of sovereignty and the death of the old year at the beginning of winter. Yews were planted profusely in medieval times to mark the boundaries of Christian churchyards. However some may have already been existent, because churchyards were often built over the top of ancient sites.

Several millennia earlier in the Bronze Age, sacred sites had burial mounds with Yews always planted to the north of them. Later, around 3,500 to 3,000BCE, they were planted on an east-west axis and, later again, Anglo-Saxons planted Yews on the south side of their sacred sites.

Yew's ritual associations may well be related to the fact that, in hot weather, the tree exudes into the air around it a resinous vapour with psychoactive properties. Spending time beneath the Yew's canopy and breathing in this vapour may well have aided the mind state of the participants during shamanic rituals. [14]

House spirit

Globally, houses have been considered to be imbued with spirit. For some, houses are the navel or axis mundi of the family, with navel posts in the centre of them providing an anchoring point for their power. In Indonesian south Sulawesi, a *Lord of the House* of the Buginese people, known as Ampo Banua, hovers around this central post as its protective house spirit. In Russian and Slavic folklore the house spirit - the *domovoi* - was said to become attached to a family. When they moved house their domovai was traditionally encouraged to move with them.

Elsewhere we find the custom of structural timbers in homes being carefully positioned by builders, keeping the same orientation that they had when alive, with the root end of the timber used for a house post 'planted' in the ground to reassert its living qualities.

To not offend tree devas or harm the energy of the home, the Vietnamese Jorai tribe acquire for building a tree from the forest only with careful ritual to appease the dryad and prepare it for a new life in the home. Invocations are chanted to these wild spirits, appealing them to become domesticated and benelovent. [15]

Across Europe the front doors of sturdy homes were once made of stout timber such as Oak. It was this wood that is thought to have

Above: A door in the medieval village of Lohr am Main, Germany

been the origin of the resident house spirit. From previously tending to its tree, the tree deva turns its attention to providing protection and care of the home and occupants.

Fascinating communications with such a house spirit have been related by Verena Stael von Holstein. Miller, as he liked to be known, was the chief house spirit of the old German mill house. He started life as an Oak dryad in the 13th century. Later, his tree home was harvested for timber and his wood incorporated into the mill house. Thus evolving into a house spirit, his work then became focussed on checking the health of the mill house's timber frames and co-ordinating the household duties of other devas. Miller, who came across as highly intelligent, was very fond of the mill owners and keen to explain about devic life. [16]

Irish *Fairy Bushes* and haunted trees

As well as possessing an individual dryad and interacting with related plant and land spirits, trees can harbour a range of other spirits under their generous canopies. Various devas might find sanctuary beneath them, just as humans once enjoyed under their local sacred trees.

In Irish folklore one often hears about *Fairy Trees*, otherwise known as *Lone* or *Gentle Bushes* or *Fairy Thorns*. (The term 'gentle' being a corruption of 'gentry', meaning the 'good people of the land'). Across Ireland, where fields are bare except for solitary specimens, folklore has long warned of removing these trees and the dire consequences of doing this. Not even dead wood was removed from beneath them. They were often said to be meeting places for fairies (who were also known as *Them*, or the *Other Crowd*, the *Sidhe* - pronounced shee, the *Good* or *Wee Folk*). Or they were said to be places where rival fairy tribes would fight. Such trees, functioning as portals to the fairy realms, were not to be meddled with!

Hawthorn (Crataegus monogyna and C. laevigata), also known as Whitethorn or just Thorn, has been long regarded as the most important sacred Fairy Tree of Britain and Ireland, as was Alder (Alnus glutinosa) to a lesser extent. Haw (seen overleaf in flower) provided nutritious new leaves and berries for the Neolithic diet and it has long graced the May Day festivities of spring. Often called the May Tree, its white blossoms

adorned garlands and wreaths and it was associated with White Goddesses and fertility. Roman people placed twigs of it above doorways for protection, while the Irish planted it close to their homes for the same reason. In some parts of Ireland, the first milk from a newly calved cow was poured beneath a Hawthorn tree as an offering. Taking Hawthorn flowers indoors is traditionally considered to bring bad luck. Perhaps the fairies resent thieving from 'their' tree?

Still to this day, the occasional Fairy Thorn is threatened by new developments, workers have refused to fell it and a compromise has had to be found. For instance a public housing estate near Sandy Row in the heart of Belfast in the early 1980's had to be re-designed and a playground built around a Fairy Tree, as workers refused to destroy it. The resulting Fairy Thorn Garden has wooden mushroom seats and murals of fairies painted on its walls. In County Clare in 1999 a highway bypass had to be modified to avoid a Fairy Thorn in its path, amid much media attention, with even the New York Times carrying the story. [17]

The Lone or Fairy Thorn is not to be mistaken for other categories of

Right: Irish Clootie (Rag) tree at Tobernalt Holy Well, Co. Sligo.
Below: St Kierans Tree, Co. Offaly, a famous Clootie Tree, a Hawthorn still visited on annual pilgrimages to the site of the monastery of Seir Kieran.

sacred tree or bush, such as the *Rag* or *Wishing Tree*. While a Fairy Tree must not be touched, the *Clootie* (Rag) *Tree* is found beside a great many of Ireland's 3,000 odd Holy Wells that have long been visited by people seeking cures for various ailments. Festooned by pilgrims with strips of rag and religious objects, the idea is to symbolically leave behind one's illnesses, from toothache to insanity, in the tree. The ailments ease as the (originally bio-degradable) cloth disintegrates. If a person is bed-ridden, someone else could try for a cure by bringing a piece of the sick one's bed sheet or pyjamas. Some rituals had one first bathe the ailing body part in the waters. If you didn't need a cure you might ask for a wish to be fulfilled in the same manner.

There are also other trees known as Wishing Trees that have no association with Holy Wells. Wishing Trees on the Hill of Tara have been festooned with all sorts of non-biodegradable objects by people mistakenly. These began to weigh down the branches and upset the trees, local people and the fairies, and necessitated a big clean-up. The age-old tradition there was to go and put your hand on each tree and ask for whatever you needed, but not to leave anything behind. [18]

Occasionally, significant Irish trees have been associated with death and the spirits of people. Some were used for burials of babies who had died without baptism. Others were believed to be haunted by people who had been hung from them, or other such unsettled spirits. A woman explaining why people avoided going too close to the *Pookedy Bush* in County Mayo, especially at night time, said that "As the people hanged didn't have the last sacrament, the spirit might still be wandering."

So this was another class of trees in Ireland that were to be avoided and left alone, as seen in enduring names on old Ordinance Survey maps such as the *Wicked Tree, Pooky* or *Pookedy Bush, Dullow* and *Bogle* or *Bogie Bush*. One such was the Wicked Tree near Williamstown, County Galway. This was a large Ash tree growing on a low mound, said by a local resident to have "peculiar branches on it, most unusual, bent and old lumps on it, like a big rash... Parents would say, the 'Watch out for the Wicked Bush'.... no-one would touch it. People would freeze before taking wood for the fire from it." However a search for the tree in 2012 found it had been completely removed a few years previously by new owners, as such traditions are being rapidly forgotten in today's Ireland.
[17]

It sounds as if the Wicked Tree was affected by geopathic stress, with local detrimental energies responsible for the bad reputation. Such a place would be energetically harmful for people and a portal for spirits of a kind that are best avoided. But on the whole, the devas associated with plants in tradition have brought humanity abundance and prosperity, and they were greatly respected, loved and venerated.

Not all significant Irish trees are very old. Many are the young replacements for sacred trees that have perished. Others that are still visited on religious occasions in Ireland today are just dead stumps of the original trees preserved there.

One is hopeful that the tradition of planting new Sacred Trees can be revived again across Ireland, bringing back some of the magic and wisdom of treedom.

Above and overleaf: Sacred tree stumps visited by pilgrims
on St Brigit's Day, February 1st, in Oughteragh,
County Leitrim, Ireland.

Encounters with forest devas

Forest devas in the form of giants are found across the the forested regions of the world. In Russian and Slavic folklore the *Leshy* (or *Lesovoi*) is the chief nature spirit in a forest, one who looks after all the plants and animals in it. Usually regarded as having a masculine, humanoid form, these Leshies are said to have wives called *Leshachikha* and sometimes also children (*Leszonky*). Across Russia, Croatia, Poland, Czech, Serbia and Belorussia, each forest has its own Leshy family. In Germany, the *Huter-Geist des Waldes* is the guardian forest spirit, living mostly in the oldest trees. In Latvia he might be called *Mezhsargs* and in Lithuania, *Mishko velnias*. Country people would respectfully refer to the Leshy using only honorific titles, such as *He*, or *He himself*, the *Forest Master*, or *the honorable* or *righteous one of the forest*. (Wikipedia)

In Slavic lore Leshy has been described as having a humanoid shape with bluish cheeks, green eyes and a long green beard. But he is also a shape shifter and may manifest as an old man in a sheepskin coat, or as a mushroom, a wolf, bear or raven or other being. He towers up to tree top level height. In early October he temporarily 'dies', but revives in springtime, when he becomes wildly behaved and dangerous, wandering the forest shrieking with rage at his confinement over winter and causing stormy spring weather. People were careful to keep on the Leshy's good side, or he might cause them to become hopelessly lost in the forest. When collecting firewood or hunting in his domain they would always leave an offering of salt, bread or milk. [11]

The Leshy, who might carry a magic golden rod, has been regularly seen by country folk. Encounters were recorded by ethnographers, with one account from an old woman in Kaluga Province who witnessed a forest fire. The Leshy, she said, who was as "tall as a belltower ... strode along behind all the beasts of the forest - bears, elks, squirrels and hares - who were pouring out, not in chaos, but in orderly groups of their own kind, confident that their master was in charge of his flocks, a heavy whip over his shoulder and a horn in his hand." [19]

In Scandinavia, where forests abound, these chief devas are called *trolls*. Regarded as highly evolved beings, they care for woodlands and all residing in them. In Sweden, dowsers that the author met told of how they regularly interact with trolls and help them to cope with electromagnetic pollution, that so hurts the deva kingdoms. [20]

Observations of other types of forest beings by Hodson give us some vivid descriptions. He observed one presiding over a half acre wood in Lancashire, UK, from a lofty position in the air above it. Of "considerable development" and glorious to behold, it's colours were predominantly carmine and gold. It's aura "spreads out in a wonderful ovoid of brilliant hues...for some hundreds of feet above the ground: it radiates and scintillates like the aurora borealis, while the lower portion, which enfolds the wood, sweeps down in graceful curves... Occasionally it directs the flowing forces by movements of its arms... presenting one of the most beautiful and extraordinary sights." [1]

Hodson also described the major deva of a fir forest near Geneva, Switzerland that he observed in 1924. "He seems much more familiar with mankind than most devas and communicates quite easily. It seems to be specially characteristic of this country that the human and deva kingdoms are exceedingly close together: I feel that the devas are less remote and that communication is easier," he wrote.

"He is showing me a little of his work," he goes on. "He has the faculty of expanding his aura to a very great extent, so that he can include within it numbers of the trees. He places himself near them, draws into himself, by a process rather like deep breathing, a special quality of natural energy, concentrating his aura round the group of trees upon which he wishes to work, and then releases his force, with a highly stimulating effect: this quickens the activity of the nature spirits, and stimulates and arouses the developing consciousness evolving through the trees." [1]

The first forest spirit that the author met was in August 2006 on Mount Sleza in southern Poland. This has been a sacred place since Neolithic times, where a sun deity was once revered. A pair of carved stone bears found at the summit are now kept in a church there (seen below).

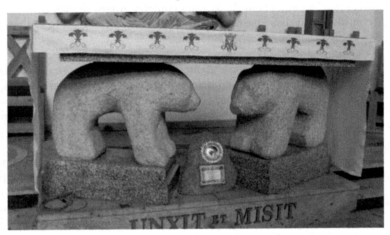

We met a local geomancer who took us up the mountain to a high energy spot. Stopping at a lookout, I found myself going alone back up the track a short distance to the edge of the forest. Here I immediately became aware of a giant (tree-height) of a masculine nature spirit that seemed to be waiting for me. I was awed by its size and power of benelovence. I didn't know anything about forest spirits at that time.

The deva was of a humanoid form, but more roundish, rough and leafy looking. We exchanged greetings and it was friendly. It even gave me a gift. I saw and felt it come close and gently present me with a cloak that it placed around my shoulders. A green cloak made of tree leaves. I felt greatly honoured by this beautiful mantle that felt so protective. But I didn't realise it's significance for a long time. I now believe that at the same time I was also being given a small forest deva. It stayed with me, quietly attached to my aura, like a totemic being. This Polish Leshy, although I wasn't at first aware if it, has been helping me with my geomancy work and whenever I've wished to meet up with devas, he has helped to arrange it. He must have also been a strong guiding force in the researching and writing of this book over the last few years.

Realising this, following some devic prompting, I tuned into my deva helper and discovered that ten years of service was long enough and with the book close to completion, his mission was accomplished. He was aching to get back into the woods! I have now installed him in my newly planted woodland in Ireland (as seen below) and he is delighted! Since forest cover in Ireland dropped to a mere 1% around 100 years ago, there must be very few forest spirits left. I have never met one in Ireland before and they may be virtually extinct. But now there is a Leshy and one day it may sub-divide and there will be more Leshies to help care for other new woodlands being planted.

Messages from the Waldgeist

Lately the author has been introducing forest spirits to dowsing students. This has happened in the Alps of Bavaria and even in a backyard in Darmstadt, central Germany. They were perceived as giants in human form, some ten metres tall and of male gender, that sometimes danced with joy at our encounter. (I was told that there were female ones, but have yet to meet them.) They were friendly and happy to communicate, often telling me, with joyful pride: *This is my forest!*

One of these fabulous giants met with us at a workshop in June 2016. Of a benevolent nature, many in the group felt rather overwhelmed by his radiance of power. They asked for a message from him and those received were varied. Some were shared.

Care for the forests.
Take care of us such as you would care for yourself.
In harmony with mutuality.

Look how ill you are, how ill that nature is.
All is hurting. Turn back to harmony.

Another percipient was told by the forest spirit that:

All the good energy given by the group was much appreciated. It would be taken and distributed to other parts of the forest that needed it.

He added that:

People should bring the energy from this woodland to other areas, to cities like Frankfurt, where it is missing.

Our high energy experience was not so surprising, given the location in a garden surrounded by woodland and a wildlife reserve. Nearby there is an energy power point, a Mother Mary grotto shrine where goddess activations have been performed. The divine female energy there was beautifully balanced by the male forest being.

Chapter three:
Herbs, fairies and healing

Chapter three:
Herbs, fairies and healing

"Plant spirit medicine is a magico-religious rite in which
plant gods bestow their grace."   Eliot Cowan

Shamanic herbalism

Original knowledge of plant medicine was discovered empirically by unsophisticated shamanic healers of the distant past. How did they amass their incredible body of practical wisdom? It was without laboratory equipment or funding. The healers surely couldn't have just guessed, or used trial and error to find their cures? They had nothing but their wits, senses and memories. With these, they created a cultural paradigm that viewed the world as alive and embued with spirit.

Traditions of shamanism explain the origins of their medicines. The medicine man / woman of the clan is the intermediary between the worlds, navigating the other dimensions of nature. Legends speak of journeying to spirit worlds and of connecting with the spirits of plants, especially those with gifts of healing and wisdom. The receptive state needed for this journeying comes with altered states of consciousness. Seen as a shift to the lower brainwave frequencies, this they achieve by meditation, drumming, extended ritual, fasting, psycho-active drug taking and the like. Whatever the method used to 'lift the veils', the results are very similar, when comparing the reports of anthropologists.

In his book 'The Cosmic Serpent', Jeremy Narby tells of his stay with tribal people in the Upper Amazon in South America. He was awed by their vast knowledge of over 50,000 medicinal plants. Asking them how they obtained this knowledge, they told him that the plant spirits had provided the information directly to the shamen. [1]

Narby joined an Ayahuasca ritual, which he was told would aid communication with the spirit world. After taking this powerful psycho-active herb, he met twin serpent spirits. Confounded by his experience, he spent years afterwards studying human consciousness. Eventually he developed a theory that these serpents could be signifying the consciousness of DNA and representing subtle communication between our DNA and that of the plant world.

The tradition of working with plant spirits to divine a herbal cure was 'rediscovered' in the early 1990's in Mexico and the USA by Eliot Cowan, who went on to become a practitioner of 'plant spirit medicine'. In his book on the subject, anthropologist and herbalist Cowan describes techniques of herbal healing that involve invoking the assistance of plant spirits. [2] He thought he might have invented the technique, but later met shamen who had been using parallel methods taught to them by their elders. Cowan was eventually initiated into Huichol shamanism in the Siera Nevada region of Mexico, where these unconquered First Peoples have maintained their traditional culture since time immemorial.

Cowan describes the unique methods of several herbalists he met. In Mexico, Modesta Lavana Perez treated his friend by praying over him and rubbing fresh herbs into his skin. She confirmed to him that it was the spirits that did a lot of the healing work, but the healer had also to rub the juice of the plants close to the important organs of the body.

Cowan then met don Lucio. This man was different. "I do my work purely by intention" he told him, pointing to his forehead. Don Lucio had been struck by lightning as a child and he then spent three years going in and out of consciousness in a coma. During this time he was instructed by spirits of nature and went off with them astral-travelling the world.

In explaining his own technique, Cowan said that "the main thing is to get permission of the spirit that is going to help me help others. If I can make that relationship with the spirit of the plant, I don't need the leaf or the root of whatever". Originally Cowan administered herbs to patients in homeopathic form and he also experimented with radionics and flower essences. However the US Food and Drug Administration banned his preferred homeopathics. So he took up an offer of help from the Storksbill plant spirit, who agreed to act as a go-between, summoning other plant spirits for him. Nowadays Cowan simply asks the messenger plant to bring the appropriate spirits through his hands into his patient's body. But he finds all methods effective to some extent, while the best herbs to work with are those that grow where one lives, or those growing in special places of spiritual power, he finds.

In the West African country of Togo, training for herbalists can take as long as twenty years. Cowan was told of healers there capable of amazing results, of eliminating conditions such as diabetes, which is considered incurable in the West, as well as heart disease, cancers and others. To discover how a medicinal plant might help them, they go into altered states (by trance or drugs) and certain sounds are used to invoke the spirits of each plant, by either the voice or drumming.

"Plant spirit medicine is a magico-religious rite in which plant gods bestow their grace," he concluded. "How is that grace invoked? Some people use song; others use pills and potions; still others lay on hands, wave feathers, or dance. Who knows how many ways may be waiting to be discovered or rediscovered?" [2]

French herbal maverick

In his time, Maurice Messegue was one of the greatest of modern herbalists in not just France, but famed right across Europe. His cures were simple, but they often had miraculous effects on people who had been given up on by their doctors. At the peak of his career he was consulted by the likes of Churchill, Rockefeller, Cocteau, Farouk, a French president, top military people, plus stars of the stage.

In his autobiography, Messegue speaks of using a pendulum and dowsing for remedies. This natural, down-to-earth countryman had nothing to lose with his honesty, as patients were plentiful, bringing him great fame and fortune. An unschooled peasant healer, he had great love for the plants that he collected in the wild places, where they grew much better and stronger than in cultivation. Messegue also acknowledged that herb lore was originally acquired from plant spirits. [3]

Irish herbal fairy lore

It was common knowledge in Ireland's past that various species of nature beings inhabit the world on spiritual dimensions, just as we inhabit the physical world. Fairies were said to live in groups or tribes, with a *fairy queen* or *fairy mistress* ruling each "house or regiment" of them. A queen or king also ruled each plant species. These plant devas were consulted by and assisted fairy friendly individuals, the *fairy doctors* of old. When such a healer gathered a plant, Lady Gregory was informed over a century ago in Ireland's west, they called upon the king or queen of the plant, who would be "kind and gentle, and whatever you'll ask them for they'll give it," she was told. "They'll do no harm at all if you don't injure them." [4]

The appearance of the fairy queen has been described as a glowing human-like being with a golden crown on the head, while the *fool* (in Irish - the *Amadan na Briona*) has been said to look like a very large, half naked man; or as a "sort of clown", or as a shape shifter sometimes looking "like a youngster...[or] the worst of beasts". Shape shifting being a common attribute of nature beings.

Sometimes people were said to be *away* with the fairies. A cure to bring them back was to "get the leaves of the lus-mor [mullein, seen right] and give them to him to drink," Lady Gregory was told by a healer. Many fairy doctors specialised in cases where the patient was given a *touch* or *stroke* from a fairy. One imagines that the fairy wand bestowing goodness and light depicted in Victorian era, sickly sweet images, also delivered the punishing stroke! Curing the stroke of a queen or the *fool of the forth* was considered the most difficult challenge for a healer. [4]

(A forth, pictured overleaf, is also known as a fort, rath, liss or fairy fort. These are the numerous circular banked earthworks, the homesteads of Iron Age times, that became wilderness zones, ideal for fairies to reside in after their human inhabitants had died or left).

It wasn't just any herbs and plants that were used medicinally. The location where they grew was considered important as well. Rev O'Hanlon wrote that "herbs and plants in raths or dells are collected with various kinds of mummery and used for charms and cures by 'bone

setters' or 'fairy doctors'. These herbs are considered specially impregnated by some mysterious fairy influence, efficacious for the healing art... Sometimes the 'fairy man', also known as a 'charmer' or 'cow doctor', undertakes to remove fairy influences from sick cattle, by some prepared herbs, and nostrums performed at a spring well. He will not allow anyone to approach during the progress of his operations," O'Hanlon reported. [5] The mixing of herbs with pure spring water at a special well was a common practise of herbalists.

At herb harvesting time, magical procedures and invocations were once used and these link back into the fairy doctors' Druidic heritage. In Gaul/France Druids wore white clothing when harvesting their medicinal plants, Roman writer Pliny wrote. No doubt the intention was to invoke a pure state of being in order to better access the invisible realms. [6]

Herbs were often picked before dawn and certain days of the week were assigned for picking them. But it was an individual thing. "Sunday evening is the best time to get them", Mrs Quaid told Lady Gregory "and I was never interfered with. Seven 'Hail Marys' I say when I'm gathering them and I pray to our Lord and to St Joseph and St Colman. There may be some watching me, but they never meddled with me at all." [4]

These activities were barely tolerated by the Church, so fairy doctors were careful to appear to work within a religious framework. Sometimes priests became fairy doctors, but they risked prosecution and some had to spend time in special gaols for their unsanctioned curing work.

Below: Comfrey, also called Knitbone, is a powerful medicinal herb.

Biddy Early

The most highly acclaimed of the Irish fairy doctors and seers was Biddy Early of County Clare. "Biddy Early surely did thousands of cures. Out in the stable she used to go, where her *friends* met her and they told her all things," an informant of Lady Gregory said.

"The priests were greatly against Biddy Early," said another, "and there's no doubt it was from the fairies she got the knowledge." Another explained that she was "a red, red woman". The classic red haired, wild witchy woman stereotype links back to powerful female ancestors and goddess lore of Ireland's ancient past.

One of Early's favourite remedies was made from moss growing between the two wheels of the water wheel on the mill at Ballylese. For Early, this remedy could "cure all things brought about by *them*", except for the stroke given by a fairy queen or fool.

Fairy herbal traditions are rich in Ireland, but they are, of course, not exclusive to there. As Lady Gregory was informed - "There's no doubt at all but that there's the same sort of things in other countries; but you hear more about them in these parts because the Irish do be more familiar in talking about them." [4]

Welsh fairy herb doctors

In Wales the most famous fairy doctors were a family associated with a mountain lake, Lyn-y-Fan-Fach in the mountains of Carmarthenshire. This lake was the legendary home of a beautiful fairy woman. A young cowherd fell in love with her and pursued her affections, the story goes. Eventually they married and had three sons. When he accidentally broke a promise to her she went back into the lake, taking all their fairy livestock with her.

The three sons of the 'lady of the lake' often went there to look for her and one day she appeared to the eldest. She told him that he and his family would become herb doctors. She went on to teach him herbal medicine lore at nearby Pant-y-Meddy-gon, the Physician's Dingle. The family became known as the Physicians of Myddfai and their valuable knowledge was passed down through the generations. They became famous for their cures across all of Wales and beyond. [7]

The herb Tansy.

Ireland's ancient herb hospitals

In Ireland there are records of herb hospitals going back to Iron Age times, between around 500BCE and 500CE. The Iron Age was a turbulent era of invasions and tribal warfare. To heal injuries they used the medicinal herbs of the fields. Special places were set aside as *Formaoil na Fianna,* Hospitals of the Fianna, the Connaught warrior lineage, as told in ancient Dindshenchas topographical texts. They were natural places where medicinal plants grew. Formoyle can also signify a round hill, but in this context, it indicates a pleasant elevated location (above the dense forests and bogs of the lowlands) where the ill or wounded could convalesce amidst herbs of the meadow. [8]

Herbs and water taken from sacred places were deemed the most desirable to use, so it appears that formoyles were ideally located at special power places, or adjacent to sacred springs, or both. For example the hill Slieve O'Flynn in south-west County Roscommon, once the stronghold of the O'Flynn clan, was previously called Slieve Formoyle. An ancient Irish text (Laoidh an Duirn) described how Goll Mac Morna, captain of the Fianna, was seriously wounded in battle. He was escorted by one thousand clansmen to this Formaoil na Fianna and placed in intensive care there, spending nine weeks peacefully convalescing in the herb gardens and meadows of Slieve Formoyle.

This hill was said to have on it a well that was the source of the River Suck, which flows on to form a boundary with County Galway. By 1837, when topographer John O'Donovan investigated, there was no trace of a well remaining, but he did see water oozing from the hillside (from the side of an esker, i.e. a glacial ridge) that he attributed the source to. The tradition of a special well there, as seen marked on the old maps thanks to O'Donovan's enquiries, alludes to the possible site of the Slieve Formoyle hospital. [9]

The author visited another formoyle in County Sligo in 2014 and it too contained all the expected ingredients. North of Lough Arrow is a line of limestone ridges, the highest point of them being Barroe North. This strategically located townland was probably once a Bronze Age royal seat, judging by the remains of megaliths and other monuments scattered across it. At a later time it became associated with Celtic warrior tribe the Luigni (pronounced Leyney, the people of sun god Lugh). This tribe once buffered the old borders of Ulster, having been planted there by the Fir Bolg rulers of archaic Connaught after the third century AD. Celtic deity Lugh is remembered in the name for the monument - Seelewey, meaning Lugh's seat. This is, or was, a large cairn at the top of the hill. some 30 metres/100 feet in diameter, that also sports a modern concrete ordnance survey marker. An Iron Age import, Lugh is much younger than his seat, which is now in a ruinous state, having had many stones quarried from it.

In a saga originating from the Iron Age, a great battle between the gods, personified as mythical tribes, the invading Tuatha da Danaan and the indigenous Formorians, was once fought out on the elevated plains of nearby Moyturra. While they battled it out, Lugh was restrained up at Seelewey, so as not to hurt himself. Things were looking bad for Lugh's lot, so his minders let him go down to give some supernatural help. Of course they won and Lugh killed the one-eyed Balor and was made king, or top god. However other legends place Balor's death place elsewhere. So take all the medieval legends with a hefty grain of salt. However they often contain a few grains of truth, so careful sifting is required!

A formoyle of the Luigni tribe was located below Seelewey, on the lower slopes. It is accessible to the public via a sign-posted Historical Trail that traverses Moyturra. This is a delightful spot with sunny, south facing limestone terraces providing a sheltered environment with glorious views over Lough Arrow and the hills beyond, as in the photo above.

Right: Foxgloves, a heart herb, on the limestone terraces of Moyturra overlooking Lough Arrow, Co. Sligo, as seen above.

There's a magic atmosphere here and you can't help but feel great! An idyllic spot for resting and many herbs can be seen growing wild all around. In fact, it was quite a botanical wonderland to behold, when visiting the site in early summer. Tumbles of limestone pillar stones, that give Moyturra its name, were lush with tangles of delicate wildflowers, like exquisite jewels growing out of the reach of trampling cows. In a short time, sixteen medicinal herb species had been identified.

There is likely a connection between this formoyle and Heapstown Cairn, not far away, down in the valley nearer Lough Arrow. This is an enormous mound of white rounded rocks, with substantial kerb stones ringing it and likely to have a stone passage inside (it has never been excavated). At some 60 metres across and 6 metres high, it is the second highest Irish mound after the Newgrange complex in County Meath.

There is a curious legend of a healing well said to be buried beneath this cairn. In the well's herbally and magically infused waters, the legend goes, the Fianna were bathed by their healer Dian Cecht after injury, or even death, each evening of the second Battle of Moyturra. They would emerge perfectly healed the next day, able to return to the battlefront. But the Fianna's Formorian enemies learned of this and captured the well and each warrior was told to bring stones to fill up the well and close it off. This they did and the enormous cairn went up.

However, it was more likely constructed earlier than the Iron Age, as legends in Ireland tend to get updated over time to suit the political persuasion of the times. But we can get confirmation from the story that there is a strong tradition of herbal healing in the area.

A stone mound covering a well is certainly an unusual theme. As a professional dowser and geomancer, one who 'reads' the landscape energies and qualities, I was keen to pass my pendulum over the site. Sure enough, upon the summit I found the energetic signature of a 'water dome', a vortex of intense upward pressure said to denote underground water rising upwards. My pendulum spun like a helicopter, so strong was the upwelling force. It was an energetic gusher that continued upwards and I dowsed the column of energy going on to connect into a network of subtle energies in the Sky above us.

Back at Seelewey, and at a second ruined cairn lower down the hill, I was able to detect two earth vortices. These are powerful points where subtle energies can 'breathe' in and out of the Earth. As well, the ancient mound builders often incorporated alignments into their megalithic

structures and Seelewey is such a place.

The summer solstice sun sets directly behind it, in alignment with the distant cairn atop of Knocknarea, the iconic great hill of seaboard Sligo. And on the winter solstice, looking from Knocknarea, the sun rises over Seelewey. Not wonder that sunny Lugh is associated with this monument! [10]

Therapeutic Gardening

The ancient tradition of regaining health through immersion in nature and plant contact has continued through the ages, in the form of garden hospitals for healing and convalescence. A French example was described by Bernard of Clairvaux in the year 1100 AD.

"Within this enclosure many and various trees make a veritable grove which lying next to the cells of those who are ill, lightens with no little solace the infirmities of the brethren, while it offers to those who are strolling about, a spacious walk... The sick man sits upon the green lawn. He is secure, hidden, shaded from the heat of the day. For the comfort of his pain, all kinds of grasses are fragrant in his nostrils. The lovely green of herbs and trees nourishes his eyes. The choir of painted birds caresses his ears."

In the early 20th century the use of gardening as a prescribed intervention in mental hospitals was well known. In 1955 O'Reilly and Handforth were amongst the first modern day researchers to publish evidence of the therapeutic benefits for psychiatric patients. They evaluated a programme of *horticultural therapy* (as it is usually called in the UK) for fourteen women. Of these women, only one failed to show a striking degree of improvement following the programme. Despite much other evidence of successful outcomes, horticultural therapy died out in the 1960s, from the advent of new pharmaceutical treatments. It was far simpler to give patients a pill. [11]

But this new approach to psychiatry had limited effectiveness. And so, by the 1990's, Therapeutic Gardening had emerged and it is now an official modality and profession in the UK, where a one year training course is offered in Coventry. There is even a British charity for Social and Horticultural Therapy, with Thrive supporting the work of numerous local garden groups operating around the country.

It is now well recognised that gardening, whether it is an active or passive involvement, provides a host of benefits of health and wellbeing to the gardener, the sick and the vulnerable. Thrive has pointed out that an individual can burn off calories almost as fast as a session at the gym, with 45 minutes of gardening being equivalent to 30 minutes of aerobics. As well as improving physical wellbeing, physical gardening activity helps to manage mental illness. Studies show that patients involved in horticultural programmes and activities report decreased stress, depression and anxiety. [12]

Gardening, especially in group situations, can also promote social inclusion, hope, trust, nurturing, the joyful creation of beauty, an awakening of the senses and connection with the cycles of nature. Gardening provides a meaningful, purposeful activity. Without *meaningfulness*, studies reveal, activities done purely for exercise or diversion lack therapeutic benefits. [13]

Learning new skills and experiencing *flow* is another key to the benefits. Flow is a term often used in occupational therapy. It's when one gets into an almost meditative state, totally engaged in a meaningful activity and resting the mind from worries. Getting into the flow reduces stress and anxiety, and it helps people to better re-integrate the parts of themselves.

A typical therapeutic garden setting will have accessible pathways and garden beds, allowing people of all abilities to enjoy scheduled activities that are run there. There is a profusion of plants with comfortable seating to enjoy looking at them, that also allows for social exchanges. The atmosphere is benign and protective, with only natural and organic growing principles used. A hot house can provide year round use. Therapeutic landscaping ideally engages all the senses throughout the seasons, the Sensory Garden being a favourite feature.

General characteristics of the therapeutic garden were first developed in 1993 by the American Horticultural Therapy Association and they continue to stand as a benchmark for design. But therapeutic garden design is all about responding to the abilities and needs of the users, so each garden is unique. [14]

Meanwhile, regulations in the EU and USA are slowly strangling the marketing and use of medicinal herb preparations, while countries like Australia are also following suit. It is difficult to buy herbs along with any information about their therapeutic use. However herbalists continue to ply their ancient trade and there is still a huge demand for naturally grown medicinal herbs worldwide.

Above: Sensory Garden at The Organic Centre,
Rossinver, County Leitrim, Ireland.
Overleaf: Herbalist and herb grower Marina Kesso, County Sligo, Ireland,
selling her wares at a festival market.

**Chapter four:
Connecting with plant spirits**

Chapter four:
Connecting with plant spirits

"Trees are sanctuaries. Whoever knows how to speak to them,
whoever knows how to listen to them, can learn the truth.
They do not preach learning and precepts, they preach,
undeterred by particulars, the ancient laws of life."

Hermann Hesse

In the Western World, society tends to shun spiritual perceptions of landscape and nature. This is inevitable, as it clashes with the idea of nature as being a mere 'resource' waiting to be exploited. The *animistic* approach, or *pagan* view, has been warped and demonised by the dominant paradigms for too long. The word pagan simply means the 'people of the land'. Reclaiming pagan thinking can be spiritually and environmentally enriching and it doesn't have to be at odds with mainstream religion. In fact, the most well known revival of plant-human spiritual re-connection occurred within a Christian context in a bleak, windswept corner of Scotland.

The Findhorn experience

Early in the 1960's a group of four people pioneered a community near the village of Findhorn in northern Scotland. With little money to go around, the growing of food crops was of high importance to them. But the soil was infertile sand dunes, the location cold and windy. Dorothy Maclean, during her daily prayers to God for help, started to receive gardening advice from the plant deva kingdom.

Gardener Peter Caddy went on to produce astonishing vegetable crops, such as a famous 42 pound / 19 kilo cabbage and magnificent flowers, by following the advice given. Later Dorothy made a connection with the overlighting deva of the area (she called it a *landscape angel*). Then an associate of theirs, Richard Ogilvie Crombie, a retired scientist and sensitive known as Roc, introduced them to the nature being Pan, a fractal of whom (i.e. a local deva of the Pan species) lived in a wild corner of their land.

Previously, Roc had had a profound experience in his local park in Edinburgh. He had gone into an altered state of consciousness and, with highly lucid awareness, found himself being approached by a tree spirit that began to communicate with him. Describing it's appearance as a classical faun, it looked to him like a small boy with shaggy legs, cloven hooves and a pair of horns on its head. Kurmos, as he called himself, told him that he was involved with caring for the trees in the park. Later Roc encountered a larger faun-like spirit that walked beside him down the city streets, radiating a great deal of power. He soon realised that this was not a faun at all, but actually Pan, the great god of nature. This local Pan quizzed him about his reactions to it and when he declared that he felt no fear, it was most reassured. It spoke of the demonisation of Pan by the Christian Church and the sadness this caused.

Another time Roc met a Pan on the Scottish island of Iona, who told him that "*I and my subjects are willing to come to the aide of mankind in spite of the way he has treated us and abused nature, if he affirms belief in us and asks for our help.*" Roc concluded that "it became apparent that what was happening was a sort of reconciliation between the nature kingdom and man." [1]

Spirits of the herbs

For many people in Western society, inspiration gained from reading books about the Findhorn experience was an encouragement to experiment. It had raised the possibility that others might be able to connect with nature beings also. After all, didn't shamen in tribal societies do this sort of thing in their healing work? Eventually, people have become more open to such down-to-earth spiritual realities and interactions. And Western herbalists of the witchy kind, who inherit the ancient shamanic traditions, are connecting to the devas of healing plants and learning from them directly.

"A herb plant can tell you more about itself directly than any book or article", Selena Fox wrote back in 1980. "For this to happen, however, you must become its friend and give it the same kind of respect and consideration you would give any human friend," she emphasised. Fox sees herb devas as either a glow around a plant, or as a glowing sphere of light above a plant, or else as a traditional fairy being. [2]

Sensitive herbalists know that true herbal wisdom comes from forging good rapport with plants and becoming their friends. They suggest spending time with plants, growing them, caressing and talking to them, breathing in their aroma, and sending them loving thoughts and happy feelings. To listen in stillness for any messages coming from them.

"When I am in need of some herb energies for a particular condition," Fox explained, "I go out to our fields and gardens while meditating on the condition and then look around to see which of my herb friends signal me that they have help to offer. I often see flashes of light above certain plants and/or feel drawn to them." Fox asks how much she can harvest, where to take it from and how to use it as an effective remedy. After her "telepathic exchange" she always says thanks and sometimes gives plants an offering in gratitude, such as a drink of blessed water or healing energy from her hands placed around the plant.

Above: The herb Meadowsweet growing freely on an Irish rural roadside.

Flower essences

Since the 1930s in the UK, healing energies of flowers have been gathered and harnessed in the pioneering work of Dr Edward Bach. This sensitive doctor discovered how to soak or boil blossoms in pure water to eventually obtain thirty eight essences. Bach achieved great success in treating a range of psychological ills with the remedies, spawning a whole new modality for the times. Later in Scotland a Mr Alick McInnes developed his own suite of fifty two flower essences that were equally effective for the treatment of people, plants and animals. He made them by holding a bowl of water and moving it rhythmically in front of the blooms (which remained on the plant). Others have gone on to use more 'psychic' methods, such as simply visualising the aura of the healing flower as connecting up with the aura of the patient. In New Zealand, flower essence developer Peter Archer told the author in 2003 how he takes photographs of blossoms and shows these to the water to create the essence. "The time has come for new ways," Peter enthused. [1]

Nowadays practitioners are finding even more straightforward techniques. "As an Australian Bush Flower Essence practitioner, I use the flower essences daily", Kate Twomey of Brisbane, Australia, informed the author. "However, I have found that they are equally as efficient energetically. That is, *thinking* about the essence is the same as taking it," Kate said.

Plant devas are sometimes consciously invoked in the process of flower essence making these days. Machaelle Small-Wright of the Perelandra Gardens, USA, has been developing her own technique since 1984. When preparing essences she connects to the plant devas and asks them to release the flowers' balancing and healing energies into the water. Being in the right state of mind is all-important to be able to achieve this transference, she says.

The Perelandra flower essence energy balancing technique takes one hour. Peter Archer discovered ways to expedite this process so that he can achieve the same results in just a few minutes, by connecting to the devas. Results can be almost instantaneous, he told the author. [3]

Healing trees

Like a forest spirit with its magic wand, shamanic healers use wooden wands they are gifted from sacred trees and with them, harness plant spirit wisdom and healing ability. This practise no doubt has an ancient origin. But you don't have to be a shaman to tap into the healing powers of trees.

Sydney dowser, the late Isabel Bellamy advocated placing against the skin small branchlets of dowsing-selected trees for a certain time, possibly overnight, so as to absorb healing energies from them directly.

This follows ancient tradition. For example, people with rheumatic or arthritic pain would once fill a warm bed with leaves of the Silver Birch tree (right) which, when laid in, would induce heavy sweating and relief from the condition. [4]

Several homeopathic remedies have been created from trees in recent times. These connect us to the essential energies of the tree and even to the tree devas themselves, as the author discovered. When taking a homeopathic dose of the tree for healing purposes, I went on to meet the over-lighting Silver Birch Deva.

Taking a high dilution of the tree remedy, I lay down and deeply relaxed, the pill dissolving slowly under my tongue. I was surprised and delighted to clairvoyantly see (eyes closed) the deva manifesting within

my energy field. I saw her as a slender female cloaked in a shiny white Birch bark coat and mask as she leaned over me. I could feel her gentle power, beauty and refreshing qualities. She quickly went to work on me and I soon felt much better.

Later I took a homeopathic dose of Oak tree. The Oak deva came to my assistance, appearing to me as a strong man with a rough brown covering and carrying a big club, a Herculean figure no less! He imparted his strength and fortitude to me as well.

Left: English Oak.

Trees to the Rescue!
by Sharon Quigley, Western Australia

Sometimes a beneficial connection with plants can happen when you least expect it and don't ask for it. Sharon Quigley told the author about a special experience she had involving Eucalyptus trees. She was on a gruelling six hour road trip with her ex-husband, receiving verbal abuse from him for most of it, when things suddenly changed.

"I remember the moment we turned a corner to drive down another road, but this road was different, it was a very wide straight gravel road into a forest of the tallest Jarrah trees I had ever seen. The trees were breathtakingly beautiful. It was nearing the end of the long journey, and my ex-husband had finally stopped ranting abuse at me and turned up the volume on the CD player to get a reaction from me. But it didn't bother me. I was mesmerised by the ancient trees and I kept staring out the window at the tall ancient Jarrah trees and admiring their beauty.

"Then the most magical thing happened, I actually felt the trees' energy and they spoke to me. I heard the trees whispering to me, telling me not to worry, that everything would be okay and I felt my sadness melt away. It was the trees who actually spoke to me in my mind, it wasn't my own voice. It was as though a weight had been lifted off my shoulders, because I knew that the relationship with my ex-husband was over and I felt calm and happy. From that moment on, my ex-husbands' words never affected me again, it was like I was wearing an invisible shield of protection, given to me by the trees."

Music of the Plants

At Damanhur, the famed intentional community in Italy, explorations into plant sentience and communication over the past forty years have shown that plants can clearly demonstrate their intelligence in a laboratory setting. Researchers at Damanhur have now found a way to allow plants to create music! The method is based on experiments popularised in 'The Secret Life of Plants', where Clive Backster and

Paul Sauvin had attached sensitive polygraph electrodes to the leaves of various houseplants. They sought a sentient response to the administration of pain and they got it. Even the thought of someone giving pain to a plant could cause an alarmed reaction from it, they saw. Damanhur's researchers took a much more friendly approach. [5]

"The technology is simple enough: a biofeedback system takes the electrical resistance from the leaves to the root system of a plant or tree and converts it into musical notes – nothing especially interesting there", explained Tigrilla Gardenia, who has a degree in music engineering and electrical engineering. "What is remarkable is that plants actually learn how to modulate their signals in order to change the sound. With practice and exposure to music, their playing improves, allowing them to play with ever-increasing complexity and in harmony with other plant and human musicians", she wrote.

The researchers discovered that the more a plant is cared for, the more music it produces. One of them could not get his plants to sing at all. He admitted he didn't care much about plants. But then when he started being more friendly with them, the music began! [6]

Initiating tree spirit contact

Developing a rapport with a tree usually takes time and depends on your intuitive development and the occasion. The more you practise, the easier it becomes. For beginners it's a good idea to first purify yourself, letting go of any negative thinking, and clearing and strengthening the aura. (If you feel fearful in any way, it's a good idea to visualise a lattice of protection surrounding you, that will filter out any harmful energies, while allowing beneficial energies to flow in.)

Which trees to experiment with? Some trees have a well known affinity for people. European tradition has it that Oaks, Rowan, Hawthorn, Beech, Hazel, Apple and Willow are people-friendly. The less friendly trees are said to be Elder, Elm, Ash, Holly, Pine and Fig.

In Australia, many species of Eucalyptus trees plus others, such as the White Cypress Pine (Callitris glaucophylla) may be unfriendly. The latter is considered by some Aboriginals to be hostile to humans. [7]

Left: The author's husband Peter Cowman and Eucalyptus tree at the Darling River, western NSW, Australia.

However there are other stories of good connections with supposedly unfriendly tree species, so there are obviously exceptions. No need to be trapped in any tradition! Talk to the plants in your area and be receptive to what they might say to you.

The best times for this type of questing is usually when you have a strong need-to-know something, or else you might dowse for a suitable time of day.

When discovering a new plant you want to connect with, don't just rush in! Stand back and send love to it first, mingling and exchanging your energies. Tree spirits are generally slow to react to experiences, so don't expect much too soon. As Glennie Kindred puts it, trees: "have much to teach us if we slow down and ask for their guidance and help". [8]

A short period of initial meditation is a good idea. After this you can go to the tree and sit quietly near it, say hello mentally/emotionally and wait for a response. You might establish an inner connection by hearing, seeing, feeling, smelling, or simply by 'knowing'.

After establishing a good connection with a tree, you might like to try holding a few of its leaves and say thankyou heartfully. Then take the leaves in your thumb and first two fingers and consciously draw in and absorb the tree energy in through them. Or keep some leaves tucked inside your clothing and touching your skin for a while.

How do we know we are making a good tree connection? Well, sometimes things do instantly happen to give us confirmation when we need it, such as in the following account.

"I was practicing some of Marko Pogacnik's 'Hologrammic Touch' exercises," wrote Kate Wimble, of Young, NSW, Australia. "In particular, the one to send energy and love to nature beings. I directed this energy to my Oak tree. Next, suddenly, the Oak leaves on the ground started to dance leap and dance around me. There was no wind. It was as though they were playing with me. I looked to the Oak tree and we 'connected'. Yes! It was responding. We saw each other and acknowledged it."

Developing Love of Nature and the Plant Kingdom
by Dr Geo, Canberra, Australia

"When I was a teenager I became aware of the peacefulness of nature. I especially loved to walk amid trees in the suburban streets or in the Australian bush (forests). My fascination stemmed from the fact that I could observe a single leaf or frond, marvel at its detail, then stand back and be filled with joy by the overwhelming beauty of the whole tree. Also, I would concentrate (through my heart) upon a single flower, and again step back to take in the whole shrub or tree. Such methods were actually expanding my consciousness, but I never knew this at the time.

"Soon, after several long walks through nature this way, I started seeing pulsating lights coming from the trees and branches. I discovered there was great peace and love emanating from flowers or leaves moistened by rain or dew; that the trees and flowers were themselves living lights of extraordinary beauty that was beyond any words.

"One day, whilst walking in the Australian rainforest among the Ferns and Eucalypts, I began to see the energy streaming out from trees. I could, by an act of will, attract it to myself or send it on to other trees. This was, of course, a major breakthrough for my practical understanding of the energy flows. Then I was shocked when suddenly I saw 'tall slim men' of differing heights (mostly about two metres tall) all carefully watching me as I walked past. When I turned and looked

directly at them it was obvious I could see them, so they scattered back into the tree trunks. Seeing these tree spirits was the start of a great adventure in consciousness which has continued for over twenty years."
9

Tree Meditation

People have been deriving energetic benefits from trees since time immemorial. In North America, indigenous people lean their backs against the trunks of trees and, stretching out their arms, feel the tree's energy being drawn into their bodies. In ancient Rome, soldiers revitalised flagging energies by sitting with their backs leaning up against tree trunks.

The practise of plant connection by the following Tree Meditation develops the ability to sensitise to nature, while also helping to balance one's own energies. Many meditation techniques are focused on the Sky energies and don't have a grounding component. But this meditation will bring enhanced balance of Earth and Sky within us.

Sitting under a friendly tree, having gained its permission, one visualises that you are *reversing space* with it. While breathing slowly and deeply, imagine your body as the trunk, your arms as branches reaching up high to touch the Sky. Feel the sunshine on your leaves, the breeze in your branches. Visualise your spine stretching downwards through the floor/ground, becoming roots that travel deep down into the ground and spread out in all directions, connecting with other roots and fungal networks. Your roots reaching further down, deeper into Earth's core, to the fiery centre and the transformative, vitalising power there that rises up into you.

At the same time, as you breathe in, visualise that the energy your tree/body is collecting from the sun is being brought down the trunk/spine to your heart centre. Earth energy is simultaneously being drawn up the trunk/spine from deep down, with both streams meeting in your heart chakra. From this point, on the outbreath, visualise the energy radiating outwards in all directions, cleansing and revitalising your tree/self. (A knowledge of the tree's subtle anatomy is also useful for your visualisation. This information is covered in later chapters.)

Fairy Meditation

Over recent years the author has been developing a Fairy Meditation whereby one can expand the fields of consciousness to connect into the deva worlds from any distance. It allows me to check on the state of the garden devas and it's fascinating to watch their energies and emotions changing over the times and seasons, and in response to certain events. Regular practise of this meditation keeps my senses more open and alert, while exercising all the super-sensory abilities and giving the garden a good blessing at the same time.

By regularly touching the consciousness of the plant and garden deva kingdoms this way you experience how everything is energetically connected. This ability helps to explain remote viewing, telepathy and other natural super-sensory abilities. It's a great exercise for sensitising to the environment. Knowing that our mental energy fields can expand to any size, thinking can take us anywhere that is only limited by the imagination! Our astral fields can also expand to give us the ability to perceive energies 'remotely' on the feeling level and to give love to our plants directly. The illustration below is an attempt to show the intermingling of our fields with a target plant and it's deva.

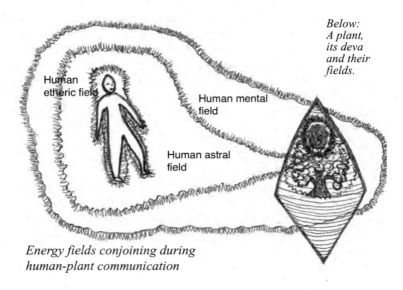

*Below:
A plant,
its deva
and their
fields.*

Human
etheric field

Human mental
field

Human astral
field

*Energy fields conjoining during
human-plant communication*

First I get into a sitting position that will be comfortable for some twenty minutes, in a place that's free of electro-smog. To begin focused and clear, and as a signal to get into the slower brainwave state of increased sensitivity, the ringing of bells, ting sha or Tibetan bowls is a good starter. Then with eyes closed and breathing pattern slow and deep, I visualise that with every in-breath I fill myself up with a cloud of golden light. On the outbreath, this light radiates out from every pore in the body to fill the room and beyond.

Below: A comfy meditation spot is a must!

I like to do further inner work before heading off into 'fairyland'. One good way is to breathe coloured energy through all of my chakras in turn, starting at the root chakra, on the end of the spine (as in the diagram overleaf). On each in-breath I visualise drawing in golden light (that comes from above, below and all round me) into the chakra and, on exhalation, this golden light then radiates out from it in all directions. This is repeated going up the spine, next with the sacral chakra (just below the navel), then the solar plexus (top of the diaphragm), heart, throat, brow and finally the crown chakra, just above the head. In the process I can note any energetic anomalies, such as lack of good flow, that my chakras might reveal and give me cause for reflection about my own wellbeing. When this has been done I find it much easier to focus and the general flow of the meditation is improved.

So then it's back to breathing the golden light into the whole of my being, including all of the chakras, then breathing it out into the world.

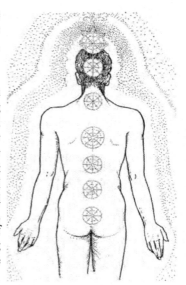

Then comes the main job. This is, in essence, the visualisation of getting out and visiting all of the special plants and places that I care for in my home and gardens. This I do area by area and I'm sort of emulating what the garden fairies get up to. In fact, I often imagine myself flying around the place, sometimes waving a wand, or sprinkling out endless quantities of gold dust or rose petals and spreading clouds of golden energy everywhere in a fairy-like manner.

This process is repeated several times with a few different colours. I usually follow the golden light with green light, during the growing season at least, as I focus it on encouraging good growth in plants. Then lilac/purple light is spread about, to help with maintaining balance and harmony. Then I finish off with radiating rose pink, for sending out love to all. (And, lastly, any distant human loved ones get the benefit of this rose colour treatment too.)

Any plant that is weak or ailing gets special attention. Important deva homes are also visited on my rounds, the residents acknowledged and honoured. I observe the devas at their stations and give them greetings, good energy and love, and sometimes a token gift, such as a flower, or some amethyst crystals. Occasionally they reproduce (sub-divide) and the new little devas are a delight to observe.

For anyone attempting this meditation who wants to develop the ability to see their garden devas, one can use the imagination and visualise what you think they look like, while keeping the eyes closed. With this visualisation practise, adventures in 'fairyland' will eventually start to happen, without even having to leave the house. And it is also excellent practise for honing one's divining ability.

Communicating with Plant Devas Summary

1. Discover, by dowsing or direct sensing, an appropriate plant that would be happy to work with you and be friends.

2. Sit beside the selected plant in a state of meditation, tune into the plant deva and say hello friend! Try to pick up any impressions of it. First impressions are usually the best ones, as they say. Or else, imagine how the deva might appear and hold the image in your mind's eye.

3. Lavish the plant with feelings of love and affection, until you feel a good connection has been made. You may feel a little jolt of energy come into you, as if a fairy wand has zapped you, or simply a lovely feeling. Ask if the plant spirit would now like to communicate with you.

4. Send the deva mental pictures (thought forms, thought packages), such as visualising how you plan to make changes in the garden. All the while be projecting loving feelings towards it.

5. Ask the deva questions about whatever you would like to find out, such as by dowsing with questions that give either a yes or no answer.

6. Discover the deva's name by dowsing, or ask to be told it. You might clairaudiently hear some sounds that suggest words. Create a name from these sounds and use it each time you communicate. It will be your point of connection, so only say the name when you are asking for the deva's presence or help. Never call them needlessly.

7. Ask if the deva has a message, or something for you. Be in an open and sensitive state to receive it. A message received may come as a flash of knowing, a vision seen, some words heard, or a sensation felt.

8. Offer thanks for the friendship given. This can simply be a feeling of gratitude projected straight from the heart. Or you might leave an actual gift, such as a flower, some bread, a glass of water or special stone that you have blessed. Or give the plant a drink of special water, etc.

Connecting and Healing with Herb Devas Summary

1. Discover by dowsing, or other attunement method, or simply choose the most suitable herb for your needs and find out where it is growing.

2. Approach slowly with respect, requesting friendship with the plant.

3. Get to know the plant. Feel it's form, touching it gently. Shower it with loving thoughts, feelings and actions. Don't rush in!

4. Ask if it would kindly help with your problem and wait for confirmation, gained by dowsing or by directly feeling the response. Or else the answers and help might come to you later in a dream.

5. Ask how, what, when and how much to harvest of the plant.

6. Ask to receive the herb deva's blessing.

7. Apply the appropriate part of the plant in either of these forms:

A. Tea
B. Homeopathic
C. Tincture
D. Essence
E. Chewed or eaten
F. Smoked
G. As incense
H. In Bath
I. Leaves rubbed on skin.
J Leaves placed inside clothing or bed.
K. Poultice or compress
L. Received energetically, by meditating beside plant,
   or via a third party with hands-on healing.

8. Give a show of thanks for assistance; for blessings, energies, healing or wisdom received from the herb deva.

9. Maintain a caring, loving relationship with the plant and its deva.

Chapter five:
Plant energies

Chapter five:
Plant energies

"In spring, when the Earth is robing herself in green, to the occultist it is as though nature forces, descending from the universe, draw forth what is within the Earth."   Rudolph Steiner, 1912.

Electrical nature of plants

Plants are energy power houses, a fact known to science for over a century. Electrical forces aid the transport of nutrients in sap to spread upwards throughout the plant. The sap flow of plants makes them electrical conductors and so a forest is a great power centre in the landscape. Acting like acupuncture needles, trees are intermediaries between Earth and the ionosphere, constantly discharging atmospheric electrical tension. The effect is stronger at higher altitudes. Because of this electrical discharging, forests help to stabilise Earth's magnetic field. There is a direct correlation between vegetation density and the strength of the field. De-forestation weakens the protective magnetic field, allowing more harmful cosmic rays to enter the atmosphere. [1]

Plants all have their own species-unique dynamic forces. These are mostly found flowing through the electrically active layers of xylem and phloem in the stem or trunk. American researcher Harold Saxton Burr proved this for the first time in the 1940s, finding trees he measured to have electrical potentials varying between 0 and 500 millivolts. Daily and seasonal rhythms, responses to dark and light, and effects from changed electro-magnetic conditions (eg solar sun-spot and lunar cycles) all showed up in fluctuating bio-electrical field strengths of the trees.

There were practical outcomes to this discovery. Around 1990, Czech researcher Vladimir Rajda found that monitoring what was now called the geo-photo-electrical currents (GPEC) made it possible to accurately assess tree health and also predict future decline. (That health problems can be detected in the energy field well before they manifest in the physical is also true for animals and humankind.) Trees may actually auto-regulate their electrical currents to adapt to the prevailing conditions and seasonal changes throughout the year, Radja believes.

Damaged trees show a significant drop in the intensity of their electrical currents, then a drop in water uptake and nutrients. Meanwhile, the electrical resistance of the damaged tree greatly increases. The tree becomes weak and unable to resist pests that might attack and easily destroy it. Radja was able to speed-up the healing of damaged plants by raising their electrical currents to normal levels, using a car battery. [1] Today many people practise *electro-culture* to stimulate plant growth and productivity, using electrical currents as well as magnets. Some people have even found ways to harvest small amounts of electricity from tree trunks!

Bees and flowers talk to each other

Electrical fields of plants are now starting to be investigated for their role in nature communication. A study from the University of Bristol's School of Biological Sciences recently discovered a form of electrical communication that occurs between flowers and bees. Bees have a high level of sensitivity to radiation, with two sensing bands around their bodies that are able to detect it. The electrical fields of flowers allow

them to communicate with bumblebees and possibly other species. "It's well known that colour, shape, pattern and fragrances allow flowers to connect with pollinators, but the new study, published in the journal 'Science', adds electricity to this already impressive line-up," it was reported. The bees build up a positive charge from flying around. When landing on a flower of a negatively charged (grounded) plant, this causes a tiny electrical discharge. The flower is thus electrically changed for a short period after the interaction and it also helps the pollen to stick to the bee's legs. For the bee, in turn, there is an improvement in "the bee's memory of flower rewards, such as pollen and nectar, affecting its later foraging pattern [and] ... they tend to keep going to one type of flower until they feel that the rewards are not worth it anymore". The study showed that "a dynamic interaction" occurs between plants and bees. [2]

The downside of bees' electro-sensory ability is their vulnerability to man-made electro-magnetic radiation, which is exacerbating general bee decline and colony collapse in the high-tech regions of the world.

Plants and cosmos

Over millennias past, people noted the effects of changing planetary and cosmic events on human behaviour and wellbeing, as well as on plants and animals. An eclipse of the Moon, for example, was known to be detrimental to seed germination, while the waxing Moon's energies can be good and stimulating for plant growth generally. Thus the science of astronomy and astrology was born. But by the 20th century, much of this knowledge had been lost in the West. Then a resurgence occurred and now science is yet to catch up!

In 1924 Austrian psychic and philosopher Rudolf Steiner spoke of the invisible life forces that link together the Universe and all living things. As his ancestors would have known, the vitality and fruitfulness of plants can be affected not only by human actions, Sun and weather, but also by the energy of the Moon and planets. Times to sow and prune, Steiner suggested in his famous agricultural lectures, should be made according to lunar and cosmic rhythms. Thus ancient beliefs were reborn in the movement he inspired, called *biodynamic* agriculture.

Many farmers have followed biodynamic systems and grown magnificent produce, thanks to its wholistic principles of sensitive soil and plant care. In Germany, Maria Thun (1922 - 2012) decided to study cosmic influences on plant growth in a serious way from the 1950s, running longstanding controlled trials on her farm on the outskirts of Darmstadt. She first discovered that planting radishes when the Moon was influenced by various constellations resulted in their growing into different shapes and sizes. Over years of research she concluded that root crops (plus onions and leeks) do best if sown when the Moon is passing through constellations associated with the Earth element. Leafy crops do best when the Moon is associated with Water signs; flowering plants do best associated with Air signs, and fruits do better with Fire signs. She and husband Matthias went on to produce, from 1962, a series of highly regarded, annual sowing and planting calendars; and later wrote a book 'Gardening for Life: the Biodynamic Way', published in English in 1999. [3]

In other research, Steiner's assertions have also been validated. Lawrence Edwards, for example, discovered extremely subtle cosmic influences that were being registered by deciduous trees in the tiny pulsations of their leaf buds. These rhythmic pulses can be charted throughout autumn and wintertime, in otherwise 'dormant' trees. (However such effects are not seen when trees are in strong electro-magnetic fields.) [1]

Plants grow in geometric forms and patterns, such as the Fibonacci number series. Often with logarithmic antenna-like shapes, this gives plants the ability to capture energies from a variety of sources. These days there are a great many more problematic energies around to consider. One wonders how Maria Thun's experiments would turn out now, since the environment became bombarded by high-tech communication waves?

Diamagnetism and Paramagnetism

Plants are known to be negatively charged and wood is a poor conductor of electrical currents. Most plants are diamagnetic, that is, they are weakly repelled by a magnet. But there is at least one exception. The wood of an Oak tree concentrates iron and is paramagnetic, as American Professor Phil Callahan discovered. Paramagnetism indicates a weak attraction to a magnet and Callahan was the first to associate this force with biological responses. [4] A stronger magnetic field is also found around the Oak, compared to most other trees. Oaks have some of the highest levels of electrical currents running through their trunks as well. Certainly this 'king of trees' is known for it's empowering, revitalising affects on people who tree-bathe beneath them.

Subtle anatomy

Scientific and psychic research have given helpful insights into the subtle energies of plants. However, it remains a little known field, ripe for more study. The author has dowsed occasionally for tree energies over thirty five years, including some investigations with students, while other dowsers have been forthcoming with their knowledge. But there is no definitive body of knowledge on the structure of the subtle anatomy of plants. So what do we know about the energy fields of plants?

In the late 20th century, photographs started to be taken of plants and seeds made with special Kirlian cameras that revealed their bio-energy fields. Seeds could thus be seen glowing with energetic vitality when they were healthy and viable. Leaves that had been partly cut off showed a 'phantom leaf effect', a glow that remained where the missing part of the leaf had been. Energetic patterns were seen to become less distinct in the Kirlian photos as plants grew older. More sophisticated versions of these cameras are these days revealing many mysteries. Russian-born physicist Dr. Konstantin Korotkov, a world leader in bio-electrography research, has developed the latest version, called the Bio-Well Camera, that uses the 'Gas Discharge Visualisation' technique. [5]

Clairvoyant observation describes the bio-field of a plant as somewhat similar to the human aura, in that it has interpenetrating layers of different frequencies and functions. Keen observers report the presence of *etheric* and *astral* fields around plants. Both have their own forms of intelligence. The etheric field facilitates the spread of vitalising forces throughout the plant and is found closely hugging it's physical self. Astral fields are more expansive and facilitate the emotional life of the plant. Plants respond to people's thoughts and feelings, as shown by the old polygraph studies, so this astral field function should come as no surprise. Many people report feeling love coming from trees, or, at other times, they sense the anxiety when forests are being felled.

Tree emotions

by Sharon Quigley, Western Australia

"One day I was driving to my country home from the city, along Roe Highway past Midland, near Perth, where there was some roadworks in progress. I could see up ahead that there was heavy machinery around, the kind used to build new roads, and the traffic had been slowed down from a double lane into a single lane. Suddenly I felt an extreme sense of sadness and loss, like the grief when someone dear to you passes away. It was incredible how strong the feelings of loss and sadness were, and I had no reason why! I hadn't seen anything to make me sad.

"Then as I drove further along the highway, I could see on the left hand side of the road, a grove of bushy Eucalyptus trees. I could sense that the deep sadness was coming from them! Then I turned my head to the right, to glance across the road directly opposite the grove of trees. I could see a large expanse of fresh sandy ground, which had been exposed by large earth moving machinery, and I knew the scenery looked different but I didn't quite know what had changed, or what was missing.

"Then glancing further to the right, I could see the biggest pile of tree mulch I had ever seen in my life, and instantly I burst into tears and just couldn't stop crying! I was feeling the intense sadness from the grove of trees on the left, which had been left behind, I was feeling the sadness from the pile of fresh mulch as well! I was feeling the energy of the trees once again! I blinked my eyes several times and thought to myself *'this is insane'* but I couldn't stop my uncontrollable tears from flowing.

"I pulled into a dear friend's house, who lived not far away, for a cuppa and a chat. I knew he would understand. I explained to him what had just happened and he said to me *'that's quite normal'*, that I was becoming more connected to nature. He was not surprised at all."

Spiral Force

Energy, time and space tend to curve and follow spiral patterns. The spiralling nature of energy is very apparent in the vegetable kingdom, where it is seen in the unfurling of a fern frond and the twisting of a vine up a tree trunk. The tips of all plant organs (stem, tendril, root, flower, stalk) describe an irregular helical course, called by biologists *nutation* (after the Latin — to nod) and by Charles Darwin *an inborn oscillation.* A dowser's model of plant energies proposed by American dowser T. Edward Ross, takes this one step further. According to Ross, all plants are enveloped by a spiral cone of force, which incorporates their *etheric blueprint.* These cones, having a 52° angle at their apex (the same angle as the Great Pyramid at Giza), are found in an ascending sequence of four, as pictured on the right.

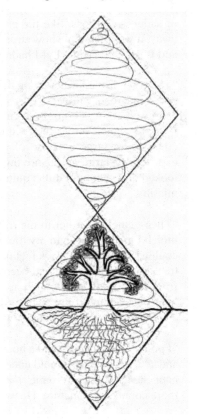

The lowermost spiral, a downward-pointing cone, surrounds the root system. The second, pointing upwards, rests on this base and encloses the upper part of the plant. Another diamond-shaped energy pattern is found attached to the first, point to point, to create a double-diamond formation. This 'quadripartite signature wave' provides two counter-rotating spins, one more active than the other. It creates a certain friction and imbalance that in turn serves to generate creative growth. The spiral energy pattern exists from seed and can be located by dowsing. [6] (Other people have described clairvoyantly seeing similar energy cones around people.)

Rudolph Steiner also alluded to ascending and descending forces at work in plant growth. "The occultist recognises - around the young sprouting plant - changing, transforming beings who have, as it were, been released from the surrounding space and penetrate downward; they do not, like the physical principle of growth merely pass from below upward, but come from above downward, and draw forth the plants from the ground. So in spring, when the Earth is robing herself in green, to the occultist it is as though nature forces, descending from the universe, draw forth what is within the Earth," Steiner said at a lecture in Sweden in 1912. [7]

Clairvoyant observer Dora van Gelder spoke of seeing two currents of energy that are drawn upon to nourish a plant. One that is coming up from the Earth below, the other coming down from above (with energies from the Sun in particular). "These two streams look like ascending and descending spirals of light in the stem of the bush," she wrote. [8]

To dowsers these spirals have been generally divined as two dimensional, flat spiral forms. For example, English dowser Vicky Sweetlove has written of dowsing a 'guardian tree', an Oak at the entrance to her home. Around this Oak she found "spirals of energy that change according to the weather, shrinking with the cold and expanding in the warm weather." Near her Fairy Circle, a special part of the garden with a magic feel to it, Vicky has dowsed the vibrance of tree auras that expand much further out than other ones elsewhere. "Some of them have been found to extend right out to my home to envelop it with a wonderful feeling," she told Michael Haxeltine, who found a general view, amongst the British dowsers he talked to, of familiarity with dowsing the 'rings' or 'bands' of energy around trees. [9]

Critical rotational position

Radionic pioneers in the UK, George and Marjorie de la Warr determined that every living plant has a *critical rotational position* (CRP) that locks them into a beneficial relationship with Earth's magnetic field. (Radionics is a sophisticated form of dowsing.) As seeds sprout in the ground naturally they twist around until locked into this CRP, helping explain why direct-seeded plants do better than transplants. It is possible to emulate nature and give new plants the best conditions for growth, by finding a plant's preferred CRP and planting accordingly. (This has nothing to do with solar orientation, where plant leaves shift their angles to be better positioned towards sunlight.)

Fundamental Ray and *Front Door*

Dowsers delving into the subtle energies of plants have written in old publications of the so-called *fundamental ray* and *front door* of plants. The fundamental ray is a key structure of the plant's aura, being its central energy axis. This vertical, concentrated stream of energy flowing up the trunk or stem has a function not unlike the human spine. Each species of tree seems to have it's fundamental ray positioned at a particular angle of direction.

Situated upon this axis line at some point on a stem or trunk is the 'front door' of a plant. Usually described as shield shaped, it's often found where branching begins. This energy portal is a receiver, an entrance point where dowsers and others experiment with sending healing energies into trees. It is also associated with the comings and goings of plant spirits. On the opposite side of the trunk is found the *back door*, where spent energies are released.

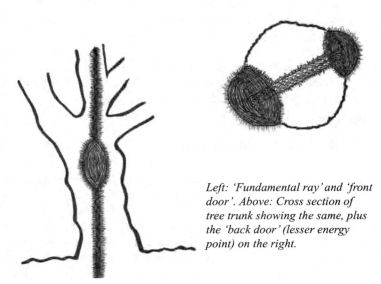

Left: 'Fundamental ray' and 'front door'. Above: Cross section of tree trunk showing the same, plus the 'back door' (lesser energy point) on the right.

96

Communication waves and lines

Plants communicate with each other in several ways, as previously mentioned. In 1989 American physicist Ed Wagner reported his discovery of another communication system. When a tree is chopped, Wagner found that adjacent trees show their alarm by putting out an electrical pulse. The chopped tree puts out a massive cry, which can be detected by an electronic probe, and the others respond to it. He called this communication mode 'W-waves', being non-electromagnetic standing waves that travel about one yard/metre per second through the trees and about five times that speed in air. These standing waves are normally just travelling up and down trees, the voltage going up and down the trunk continuously.

In Sweden in 2006, the author was shown a dowser's discovery of 'lines of communication' between trees. These are energy flows that extend out horizontally above the ground between trees, connecting them together. On checking this out, it turned out that the energy lines were emanating from the point of the front door of the trees.

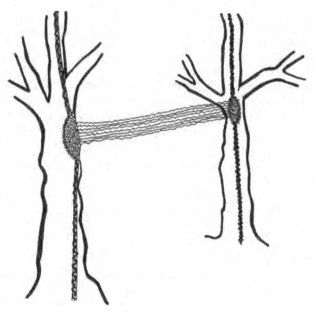

The nature of dryads

In Greek the word *drys* signifies Oak. Thus, *dryads* were originally the spirits (also called *nymphs*) of Oak trees, though the term dryad has come to be used for all tree devas attached to individual trees. Relative to most other plant devas, dryads are highly evolved beings.

"Nearly all well-grown trees have attached to them," Hodson explained, "in addition to innumerable nature spirit builders, an advanced nature spirit or a God... The presence of such a being, through the constant play of its thoughts and auric energies, greatly quickens the evolution of tree life and consciousness. Such nature spirits and Gods are subordinate to more advanced beings in charge of groups of trees of the same genus," he wrote. [10]

"The more advanced tree angels, those associated with very old and large trees, exhibit a more human clarity of mental outlook and power. Their gaze can be keen and penetrating as they turn their attention upon one who enters their realm and is able to see and communicate with them. Nevertheless, in their case also the impression is received of an intimate blending of their life and consciousness with that of the tree which they ensoul, and the evolution of which they assist," Hodson wrote.

Are the tree spirits an aspect of a tree's energy field? Not according to highly respected Slovenian seer and author Marko Pogacnik, who notes that the dryad is actually a separate being that is "on a different path of evolution" to the actual tree. Dryads co-ordinate the work of the various species of devas that associate with the tree, from the small, such as flower fairies, to the large, such as the over-lighting deva of the tree species, or Pan. [11]

Dryads can also leave their tree. This is handy if the tree has to be felled, as the deva can be re-located beforehand. When curiosity demands a good look at something that's going on, the dryad will often emerge from its tree for a short while. This is the best time that they can be clairvoyantly observed. Dryads are said to typically look like slender humans, brown in colour or sporting a colour similar to the tree's bark.

Otherwise, when inside the tree, their forms are more vague and often hard to distinguish.

Van Gelder observed dryads at night time having more time to play and relax, being off-duty from their tree care business. This is the time when they often emerge from within the trees for a wander in the woods. And so a forest at night time can be somewhat unnerving to humans and might inspire fear, although harm is not intended, she relates. [8]

Tree spirits in young trees are quite diminutive, but grow with time. They have undeveloped intelligence and only emerge from their trees when older and wiser dryads suggest to them to do so, van Gelder observed. How long do they live? When asked about the lifespan of dryads, house spirit Miller told von Holstein that they can remain active up until when the wood has completely rotted away. [12]

Tree spirits are ambivalent to most humans, however they can develop strong human connections with tree loving people. Dryads have been known to emerge from their tree to express their fondness for favourite people who might be visiting them. Tree lovers, such as Dr Richard St. Barbe-Baker and the pioneers of the Findhorn community, became magnetic beacons for the plant devas.

Man of the Trees

In Kenya he was known as the Father of the Trees, elsewhere as the Saint of the Trees and in California, the Redwood Saint. But most people know him simply as the Man of the Trees. Richard St. Barbe-Baker, an English forester turned ecologist, was a global champion of the trees, long before environmental activism became commonplace. Born in 1889 and passing away in 1982, he informed millions of people about the importance of trees and forests for the health of our planet and, as a result of his inspiration, has been responsible for the planting of an estimated 26 billion trees internationally. His work in mobilising the governments of African nations to reafforest barren Saharan fringe areas is well known. *Men of the Trees,* the association he founded in 1922, has one hundred or so branches throughout the world (it has since been renamed the International Tree Foundation). As well, St. Barbe-Baker is also considered to be one of the three founders of the organic growing movement (along with Sir Albert Howard and Sir Robert McCarrison). Knowing the imperative of global reforestation in the 1930's, St. Barbe-Baker played a key role in persuading the American government during the Great Depression to set up its Conservation Corps. Eventually involving some six million youths who were otherwise unemployed, they went out into the countryside to plant trees and perform other environmental tasks. In India St. Barbe-Baker took part in the struggle of villagers in the Himalayas to protect their forests. The Chipko (Hug the Trees) movement was mainly embraced by women, who also worked with activist Sunderlal Bahuguna to save the forests of the Himalayas. Together, they toured the region, calling upon the young men and women to fight for the trees, when St. Barbe-Baker was aged eighty eight.

St. Barbe-Baker was a profoundly spiritual man. He believed that, to save the world's forests and the planet itself, what is required is nothing short of "a spiritual renewal, a new religious world view and one very much closer to that of our forest dwelling ancestors". That we must learn once again to regard Nature as 'holy' and as a vast sentient being. St. Barbe-Baker saw nature in this light. "It is with a spirit of reverence that I approach God's creation, this beautiful Earth", he said.

Modern society tends to dismiss the view of nature as a vast sentient being as archaic and when trees cease to be seen in this way, forest destruction is inevitable. As Theodore Rozsack put it, "the de-sacralized world is doomed to become an obstacle inviting conquest, a mere object. Like the animal or the slave who is understood to have no soul, it becomes a thing of subhuman status to be worked, used up, exploited. What was previously our home, our temple, the abode of gods, and a source of poetic inspiration, becomes but a source of 'resin, timber and foreign exchange'." [13]

St. Barbe-Baker, brought up in the Christian faith, became a Bahai in the 1940s and was also unquestionably an animist. Ecologist Edward Goldsmith interviewed him in New Zealand, where he was living just before he departed on his final world lecture tour.

"Do you agree that we, in the ecological movement, must all be animists?" he asked the venerable gentleman. St. Barbe-Baker answered "Yes, that is why I so much admire the work of the people at Findhorn."

Peter Caddy of Findhorn wrote of the great man: "St. Barbe-Baker has long been aware of the presence of the devas [of trees] .... During his visit to Findhorn the Leylands Cypress Deva gave out the following message through Dorothy Maclean:

'There is high rejoicing in our kingdom as the Man of the Trees so beloved of us, links with you here.... I am speaking on behalf of all the tree devas, who have long been over-lighting the Man of the Trees and we wish to express our deepest thanks to him... He brings us hope for all the world's future. What contribution could be greater?'

Unhealthy energies

Twisted, gnarled and lumpy, or sick looking trees may be showing symptoms of living in unhealthy locations. A *geopathic stress zone*, where noxious energy emanates from the ground, such as from underground water flows, could be responsible. If a geopathic zone is too strong for a tree, it may not only become warped, but also weakened enough to become vulnerable to pests and disease, and eventually die as a result. Dowsers can check for geopathic stress. If found, then energetic changes could be made, such as by techniques of Earth Acupuncture.

The Coiled Palms of north Queensland, Australia, are affected by geopathic stress.

The ability of trees to cope with living in a geopathic stress zone can be of benefit to people. Trees are capable of absorbing or transmuting some degree of geopathic stress. If the geopathic energy isn't too strong, a tree can provide a protective screen or influence for people in the vicinity. This is why it's traditionally bad luck for a house if a 'king' or 'queen' tree in the garden is felled. [9]

We know that plants are constantly in vibratory resonance, pulsing and reacting to the rhythms of the cosmos. However subtle cosmic influences may now be negligible when compared to the strong electromagnetic fields, especially of high-frequency radiation associated with wireless transmissions, that is today ubiquitous in urban communities. Unlike us, plants can't escape this modern hazard of society.

Back in the 1980s Dr Gernot Graefe, a renowned soil and humus specialist working for the Austrian Academy of Science, was looking at the alarming decline of the forests in Europe. He noted that there were greater numbers of tree deaths along the 'Iron Curtain' that separated eastern and western Europe, especially along the borderland forest corridors where radar communications were more focussed. He acknowledged the antenna shaped tree forms, particularly of Pine trees, that facilitate the take-up of the radiation. He noted that trees were dying

Bunya Pines (Aracauria bidwillii) at the Bunya Mountains, Queensland, Australia.

from the top downwards. Graefe concluded that this and other forms of radiation, from nuclear testing and accidents, from power lines, plus increased roentgen radiation from the Sun (due to a reduction in the ozone layer), were all weakening the trees and making them more susceptible to diseases and pests.

The negative outcomes may well have been anticipated by US officials who knew the hazards of radar (radio-frequency radiation) exposure, from once-classified studies compiled for the US Navy in 1971. [14] The military went on to develop electro-magnetic weapons, often with the same frequencies, such as 1800 MHz, that were used by mobile and cordless phones in later times. These were tested on Russian embassy staff in Moscow and the protesting women camped on Greenham Common in the UK, some of whom still have ongoing health problems. By 1976 the Soviets had enough research to report well-documented health effects of 900MHz and 1800MGz frequency radiation.

In 1996 a study of health and environmental effects around a radar facility in Latvia found growth reduction and death of Pine trees up to four kilometres away from the site. [15] Forest dieback around radar stations has also been reported from northern Canada, in Oak forests north of Vienna and near Wasserkruppe and Frankfurt am Main in Germany, with lines of trees dying between the transmitters. [16]

More time have since passed, with missed opportunities to staunch the spread of wireless transmissions, so these sort of problems have worsened. The spread of radioactivity from the nuclear melt-down in Japan's Fukushima is still out of control; while the ozone hole in the southern hemisphere was the biggest ever seen in the summer of 2015. And since Graefe's time, electro-magnetic pollution levels in the atmosphere have skyrocketed exponentially.

Electro-smog effects

Electro-smog is a general term for electro-magnetic pollution of the various frequencies of (non-ionising) radiation. Levels of the higher frequency radiation range, the radio (RF) and microwaves, have escalated alarmingly in the last decade. Human exposure to electro-smog has been linked to problems such as increased stress, brain fog, insomnia, autism, cancer, lower sperm count, Alzheimer's disease, behavioural issues and developmental delays, and DNA damage. (Effects vary between the different frequencies.)

Recent research into effects of electro-smog on the environment has also shown alarming scenarios. These include plant die-off, drastic declines in amphibian populations with an increase in deformed amphibians, reduced bird populations, increased bird aggression and an alteration in the behaviour and physiology of bees. [17]

In Holland, researchers believe that electro-smog is having serious affects on city trees. A few years ago officials in Alpine aan den Rijn noticed increased malformations in local trees. A study by Wageningen University determined that wi-fi signals could very well be responsible for the diseased trees, which had bark tears, bleeding and leaves prematurely dying. Alarmingly, they discovered that 70% of all trees in the Netherlands' urban areas had these symptoms, compared with only 10% of them five years previously. The Dutch team experimented by exposing twenty Ash trees to varying levels of radiation over three months. Trees that had the closest proximity to wi-fi networks suffered from symptoms of radiation sickness, including a lead-like shine on leaves, caused by deteriorating outer-cell layers and leading to premature death of the foliage.

These tree abnormalities are an issue throughout the Western world, the researchers noted, while trees in non-urban locations are not so affected. British biologist Dr. Andrew Goldsworthy is also alarmed by the increase in mystery tree deaths occurring throughout urban areas across Europe. He found that affected trees "also show abnormal photoperiodic responses. Many have cancer-like growths under the bark (phloem nodules). The bark may also split so that the underlying tissues become infected. All of these can be explained as a result of exposure to weak RF fields from mobile phones, their base stations, wi-fi and similar sources of weak non-ionising radiation," Goldsworthy said.

American researcher Katie Haggerty, in a 2010 paper in the International Journal of Forestry Research, described her study of the influence of RF signals on Trembling Aspen seedlings. Seedlings exposed to RF signals showed necrotic lesions and abnormal colouring in leaves, she found. Meanwhile, seedlings that were shielded in a Faraday cage, which prevents RF radiation from entering, thrived as normal. [18]

An experiment devised by Dutch school girls involving seeds sprouting beside a wi-fi modem gave similar results and was widely publicised at the time. Then, in another scientific study, researchers from Belgium and Sweden exposed two groups of cress seeds to different levels of RF radiation. The seeds exposed to the lowest levels of radiation (2-3 μW/m2, or micro watts to the square metre) grew normally. But those exposed to 70-100 μW/m, which is typical of the output from mobile phone base stations, failed to germinate. When the more highly exposed seeds were moved to a lower intensity field, they began to germinate after two days. The authors concluded that "the prodigious wireless technology may affect and seriously impact nature". [19]

Businesses profiting from electro-smog will not concede that there are any hazards for as long as they can get away with it. Scientists follow the money. This already happened with the asbestos and tobacco industries. But anyone can see for themselves whether this technology is safe for life-forms or not by setting up simple experiments, such as those previously described.

An anecdotal example by the author was unplanned. A small Sage and small Rosemary plant bought from a supermarket were put into larger pots and placed on a windowsill. The spot was close to where a wireless modem operated each day for up to an hour. They stayed there for two months in springtime, the modem switched off when not in use.

As the photo overleaf shows, the two plants failed to thrive and their leaves started to look sickly. The Sage attracted a lot of insect pests to itself. They both had to be moved to a hothouse to convalesce, surrounded by other healthy plants, over another couple of months. After that time, the Rosemary finally stared to send out healthy new shoots. But the Sage died.

Chapter six;
Dowsing plant energies

Chapter six:
Dowsing plant energies

"Dowsing is an expansion of lucid awareness, in essence - familiarity in communication with the Universal Intelligence." Dr Edith Jurka

How to discover and communicate with the other dimensions of nature, the invisible worlds of energy and spirit? For anyone curious enough to try, gaining knowledge directly from the plant kingdom is not difficult. You don't have to be 'gifted'. Just allow your natural intuitive faculties to unfold, with regular practise. Then your extra-sensory development will reward you with increased clarity of perceptions. You will be able to see nature with completely new eyes!

Dowsing can be a brilliant way to make sense of the invisible dimensions and using it can give practical outcomes in the garden. Dowsing is also called divining, water witching, questing and other terms. It is an amplification of our extra-sensory perceptions and the harnessing of intuitive knowing, made manifest in the movements of the dowsing tool. This natural ability is associated with ancient instincts of seeking water and direction-finding. It is also demonstrated by certain animals such as elephants, while people have been using it to find their essential needs for thousands of years.

Dowsing is an easily acquired skill. The author has been a teacher of pendulum dowsing for over thirty years and rarely has one of the students not developed some degree of skill in it in a training session. One can either dowse by asking questions where the answer can be either a *yes* or *no*; or by direct sensing whatever energy you are focussing on using *Energy Dowsing* techniques.

How to dowse for questions and answers

A popular and easily learnt method of question and answer dowsing with a pendulum goes like this. Use approximately 30 centimetres of string to which you attach a pendulous object to one end. (My favourite pendulums are made from basalt and red granite stones.) Wrap the free end of the string around the forefinger of the dominant hand, leaving about 20cm of string for swinging. Get into a slowed-down state of thinking and breathe slowly and deeply. Sit or stand with a straight back. Don't have your legs crossed. When you feel relaxed, but also focussed and attentive, start to gently push the pendulum away from you, making it swing in an oscillating movement, up and down, away and towards you. Your arm should be in a comfortable position so that it's easy to do, as in the photo on the right.

Practise this for a few minutes, until the oscillating movement becomes 'automatic', then ask, out loud if you wish, for the pendulum to show you a rotation to indicate a *yes*. If you feel it pulling in one direction, allow the oscillation to become a rotation, clockwise or anti-clockwise. Then put it back into an oscillating movement and ask it to show you a rotation to indicate a *no*. This should be the opposite rotation. Generally speaking we tend to find that right handed people get a clockwise rotation for a yes, while left handed people have the opposite, with a clockwise rotation meaning no. Always go back to the neutral oscillation in between your questions. Then you have cleared the decks and are primed for the next query.

Can't get a yes or no? You can also designate a yes or no. It's just a matter of mental programming of your pendulum. Tell it to rotate a certain way to indicate a yes and no. Swing your pendulum in neutral, then yes, back to neutral, then no, and all the while focusing your mind on absorbing your message code. You might even ask questions of yourself that you know the answers for and see that it gives the proper response. If the pendulum is sluggish, you may have to give it a little push to keep it moving. A stationary pendulum is of no use to you. Keep it always moving when dowsing. Be super focussed and clear minded, but mentally detached and relaxed. Sometimes you may have to fake it to get the feel of how it should be responding. Eventually the mental programming will sink into your subconscious and the appropriate pendulum movements will occur automatically on cue.

Plant dowsing questions

Plants make perfect subjects for dowsing, they are regular sitting ducks for practise. Dowsing can allow you to 'interview' a plant about whatever you wish to ask. Having made friends with the plant, you might pose questions to it, the type of questioning that is going to give unambiguous yes or no answers. Note down results for future reference. What sort of questions to ask of a plant? Here are some suggested ones to get you started. Later, having practised with these, you can go on to intuit suitable questions on the spot, as the need arises.

* Are you happy to communicate with me?
* Are you healthy?
* Do you like the other plants around you?
* Do you like me?
* Are you getting enough / too much water?
* Are you getting enough nutrients?
* Is the soil pH to your liking?
* Is the necessary mycorrhizal fungi in the soil?
* Are you happy with this location?
* Is there enough sunlight for you here?
* Would you prefer to grow in a different environment?
* Are enough pollinating insects finding your flowers?
* Do you need other plants nearby for pollination?
* Are you a male / a female?
* Are your seeds viable?
* Have you been genetically modified?

Measuring by dowsing

Now you are bound to be buzzing to discover that plants are happy to communicate by dowsing. However, soon enough just getting a straight yes or no may not be good enough. You will want to know what degree of health or happiness your plant is enjoying. This is also going to be useful when it comes time to selecting fertilisers and combinations of inputs. You can find out the degree of improvement these may bring and compare them with alternative options. If you are doing energetic improvements in the garden, you will be encouraged to see plant energies measuring up better too.

So a method of measurement by dowsing is worth practising. The ruler method is a classic. You can have an actual ruler, or draw one up on a piece of paper, with any scale you wish. To make it easy, use a scale that is one to ten or one to twenty. One or zero will represent the worst and ten or twenty will be the best.

The way it is used is thus. With the pendulum swinging in neutral oscillation, you pose a question to your plant such as "What degree of health do you have, as expressed as a number out of ...?" As you focus your mind on the question, you run the forefinger of your free hand from the bottom towards the top of the scale. At some point along the way you want it to indicate by rotating.

As soon as you feel the oscillations start changing to a rotation, stop moving your free finger up the scale, allow the pendulum to indicate a yes and take a note of which number this is.

Dowsing for a friendly tree

To divine friendly, useful and healing trees by dowsing, you might make up a list of all the trees that grow in a certain area, such as your backyard or the local forest park. This can be used for dowsing over, asking for the most friendly one. As you read out the name of a tree species on the list, the pendulum stays swinging in a neutral oscillation and this can be taken as a de-facto no. When you reach the tree that does suit your needs, the pendulum will go into a rotation to indicate yes.

You might also want to find out comparative levels of affinity between you and each tree by using the ruler method. For example, several trees might come up for you as being friendly. So which is the best one? Dowsing this, you find out which gives the highest figure on the scale.

In the past, dowsers laboured over dowsing lists that were arranged in a semi-circular, fan shape. They had to train their pendulums to oscillate at different angles to indicate a word. This was rather awkward to do. So nowadays we don't bother with the fan shape and just arrange charts as lists of things down a page. Arranging a list in alphabetical order can help with developing familiarity with it. However, the fan chart does look nice and you can always just read out each word as the pendulum oscillates, rather than trying angular oscillation.

The following page has a sample list in fan chart format that readers may wish to practise with. It's a list of sacred trees of the Irish and British, plus a scale of affinity, to see what degree of resonance you might have with them. Thirteen sacred trees have been selected, as according to English author Robert Graves, who spoke of a thirteen tree lunar calendar, in his groundbreaking book of 1961 - 'The White Goddess'. Shamanic healers, such as Peter Aziz in the UK, uses wands of these trees to do his tree magic and healing work with. [1]

Tree aura bathing

Clairvoyant observation of the predominant color of tree auras finds that some trees have energy fields with a potential range of benefits to people

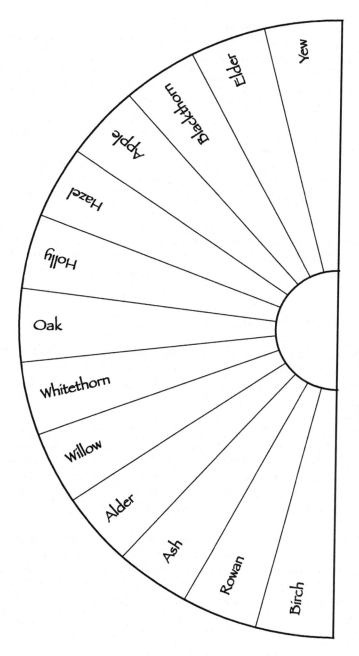

Sacred Tree Dowsing Chart

Yew
Elder
Blackthorn
Apple
Hazel
Holly
Oak
Whitethorn
Willow
Alder
Ash
Rowan
Birch

who practise 'tree-bathing'. An appropriate tree can be divined by dowsing with a colour chart, or by thinking of each of the possible colours in turn and asking about their suitability. Years ago I was told about the four main tree aura colors. (However some people may perceive these colours to be different. So this is just a general guide and you could always assign different colours if you prefer.)

GREEN aura trees can be good for general healing and also for tree-bathing under during childbirth.
BLUE aura trees benefit meditation, creativity or calming purposes.
YELLOW auras are good for learning and mental stimulation.
WHITE ones are best for cleansing and general vitalising purposes.

With *Birthing Trees*, expectant mothers become familiar with the tree for some time beforehand and communicate lovingly with it. Eventually a two-way flow of energy develops. When going into labour, they lean against the tree's trunk and feel the calming, pain-dulling influence.

Plant aura dowsing

The key to harnessing our innate dowsing ability is to develop mental clarity. And whatever we can imagine is possible to dowse! We start off by gaining an understanding of a concept, a framework of enquiry. Then we can go on to direct sensing.

To directly sense the energies of plants, Energy Dowsing, as taught by the author, can be practised with a friendly pot plant placed at around arm's distance in front of you. Energy Dowsing is ideally practised in an electro-smog free environment.To begin with, you need to focus your mind on one aspect of a plant's subtle anatomy. So let's first consider it's general energy field, the plant's aura. Think about that.

While visualising the conical form of the plant's aura, swing the pendulum in a neutral oscillation. Then, as it continues to oscillate, move very slowly towards the plant, asking the pendulum to rotate at the point where you have entered into the plant's spiral field. When you arrive at that point you might notice it wobbling a bit, so stay there and allow it to start rotating. Having developed a good rotation, then continue moving slowly through the energy field and watch the rotations. These should cease when exiting the field on the other side, with the pendulum returning back to a neutral oscillation.

What direction to have for the rotation? Well generally speaking, either direction is fine. However you may sometimes want to specifically look for a either polarity of yin or yang energy. In this case yang energy will correspond to a yes, or positive polarity rotation and yin to a no, or negative polarity rotation.

It is also good to involve the other hand when dowsing a plant aura, as on the right. While the penduling hand stays steady as it swings in oscillation, the free hand can move towards the plant in a scanning motion. You may well feel a sensation in the palm of your hand as it moves into the field, which stops when you leave it. The pendulum takes slightly longer to register the perception, by changing to  a rotation. Direct sensing with the hands can be very, er, handy! Our hands are incredibly sensitive, if we allow them to be.

Energy Dowsing develops our natural receptivity to energies. This ability is especially associated with the most highly sensitive minor chakra points in our subtle anatomy - the palms of the hands, our eyes and knees. Some people dowse with theiur eyes. And the knees as energy receivers can help explain why we may 'go weak at the knees'.

Now that the general aura has been checked, the etheric field of the plant can be focussed on. Fix your mind on the concept of this field and move the oscillating pendulum or other hand towards the plant. It will probably dowse to be somewhere fairly close to the stem. Then re-focus onto the concept of the astral field. This usually dowses to be more expansive and distant from the stem.

Dowsing the auras of trees will give a much bigger energetic response to that of your little pot plant. One finds with young trees, that their general auric field is relatively much bigger in proportion to the size of the physical tree. It could be around double the tree's size. Older trees have energy fields that are relatively weaker and smaller. As the fields provide energetic blueprints for growth, this is an understandable deterioration.

Plant energy spirals

As for the spiral force within a plant's aura, Haxeltine refers to a general concurrence among dowsers of finding bands of energy within tree auras. People have described these as two dimensional rings of energy surrounding trees and also as energy bands found spiralling vertically up trunks. The strength and size of these rings seems to be determined by age, size, season and health of the tree. [2]

How many dowseable bands might one expect to find around a tree? Shaman Peter Aziz speaks of sensing a large tree's aura, which "will have four layers, a few feet apart, with a fifth layer within the bark." [1] One imagines that this fifth band is the one that spirals vertically up and down the trunk, as in the illustration overleaf. Surely this would be an easy enough thing to confirm by dowsing. Or would it?

Having read of the four exterior bands, the author dowsed twelve different tree species, in Ireland during springtime. I also found four or five rings of energy around the trees' trunks, and also four bands spiralling up trunks. But there was one notable exception. An Irish Yew tree (Taxus baccata) was found to have twelve narrow bands around it! The particular specimen always exuded great energetic strength. But other Yew specimens did too, I discovered.

What would other peoples' dowsing find if they were not having the same expectation of finding four or five rings? When asking dowsing students at various classes in Germany in 2016 to check trees, there was a bit of variation in findings. Many people were complete novices, of course. The number of bands that they found ranged from four to nine.

Perhaps the personal element in dowsing was getting in the way. Once influenced by someone or from reading a book, one's dowsing can become slanted. Even someone's thoughts can interfere! And when our energy fields interact with plant auras, perhaps our thoughts can override the energies of the plant. I guess it's impossible to extract the observer from the observed and to not influence the result!

Tree spiral dowsing technique

Go to the trunk of the tree and ask permission to interact with its energies. When a positive reply is gained, then the pendulum is swung into an initial oscillation as you start very slowly walking away from the tree in a straight line. As you move into the inner band of the first energy ring the pendulum will change to a rotation, the direction of which reflects its polarity. The pendulum goes back to swinging in a neutral oscillation when inbetween the bands. At the second band out from the trunk it rotates in the opposite direction, due to the alternating polarities. It then returns to neutral oscillation in the gap, and so on, until reaching the edge of the tree's outermost band.

Tree chakra dowsing

When dowsing a tree's aura, the fundamental ray can be detected on both sides of the trunk. One side of it will dowse as yang, the other as yin. Somewhere along this line one can locate a strong vortex point, often found where the tree's first branches emerged. The yang side vortex is the front door of the tree, the portal for incoming energies. On the opposite side, a smaller vortex of yin energy is dowsed as negative in polarity. This back door is where energies are released.

One can also practise scanning these with both hands alone, by holding them a short distance away from a tree trunk. Divined directly this way, the energies are often felt as a tingley sensation in the palms. But on a big tree, the front door could well be too high up and unreachable.

These days one doesn't hear such terminology used much in dowsing circles. What was once called a front door is now more likely to be called a *heart chakra*, as it appears to function as a central focus of the tree's life force, it's intelligence and feelings. The place where communication lines emanate from. Dryads tend to connect to trees through this portal. We can connect to the dryad there also, by putting our head to it and sending our thoughts and feelings out.

But you may find a large tree's heart chakra too high up to reach with your pendulum. So this is where remote scanning can be used. The method is useful for dowsing anything at a distance. Dowsing as normal at a short distance from a tree, one also uses the free hand as an antenna, with the arm outstretched and pointing towards the subject. You need to be looking along the line of sight with all your concentration focussing on what is being viewed. With practise you will find that energies can be sensed from afar just as readily as if they are close to you.

Is the heart chakra the only such tree vortex? Not so, as the author found out, but it took a while to realise this. Discovering a colour painting of a tree's energies and deva, as seen by Geoffrey Hodson in his book 'Kingdom of the Gods' (depicted below, with energetic features emphasised), it was a revelation to see a lower chakra shown at ground level. [3]

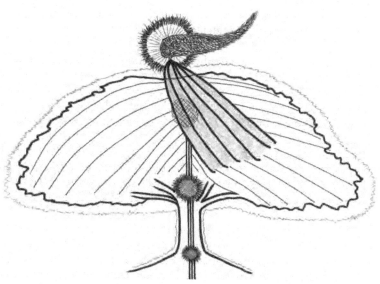

Never having looked for one there, I was excited to get out and search. Sure enough, a second chakra was found where anticipated. This, the tree's *root chakra*, is a control point for the underground world of the tree's root system. And it's also a portal for Earth elemental devas.

Hodson enjoyed observing various nature spirits interacting with plants, such as the wood elves that he saw playing around trees, sometimes forming a ring, joining hands around a tree or group of trees and merrily dancing in circles. "They seem to inhabit the roots of the trees, for I see them emerge from the roots at the level of the ground as one would step out of the door of a house," Hodson wrote. He also described a playful tree gnome that inhabited the lower section of an Ash tree. Around 75 cm/30 inches tall, the gnome lived a solitary, but happy life. It's daily activities involved providing qualities and stimuli to the tree, and it never ventured far from it. Once again Hodson mentions the mode of entering - "It is very curious to see him step into the tree at the same place and in the same direction, i.e. on the south side," he wrote. [4]

Never looking for more chakras, I was content with the idea that plants had only two. But I was in for another surprise. Truly what we don't look for, we will never find. Some students in Germany in 2014 felt that a third chakra could be lurking behind the image of the dryad in the Hodson painting and looking more closely at it, I also saw a faint point shadowing in there that I had never noticed.

Dowsing an actual tree they did, indeed, find another chakra high up and more were found on other trees. So trees have a *crown chakra*! And these are located in the top third of the tree's helical cone. (Such a location, in Egypt's Great Pyramid, another 52^0 angled shape, is the magic position of the *Queen's Chamber*). So it all seemed plausible.

Later, checking various species of tree in Ireland, I also found a third uppermost chakra located in the top section of them. Then I checked higher above the trees and dowsed indications of another three chakras. They must be in the uppermost energy diamond spirals, I guessed.

In May 2016 students in Switzerland were given the task of dowsing for the number of spiral bands and chakras on some backyard fruit trees, having been shown the root and heart chakras. Some of the students could find them and they reported four chakras. A sickly Apple tree was found to have nine spiral bands around it, yet its healthy neighbours had only four bands. Another dowsing class found four to seven spiral bands around trees and chakra numbers ranging from three to five.

One woman asked to be able to clairvoyantly see a tree's chakras and she then saw small ones located along the branches as well! Perhaps the trees' auras are similar to the human aura. In ancient Indian thought there are said to be 72,000 nadis, or lines of energy, within the human aura. Where these lines cross there are mini-vortices or chakras, some of which correspond to the Chinese acupuncture points.

We project our imagination into our dowsing search and the plant spiral force may well be highly interactive with us. But with all the discrepancies, I started to suspect I was missing something. Pondering on the lack of consensus, I went back to dowsing, guided by intuitive prompting. And then I found more chakras!

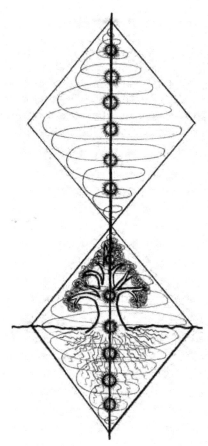

My dowsing found three chakras in each of the four helical cones, making twelve in all - nine above ground and three below. It seemed a logical pattern for the model of the plant's aura. The power of three is well known!

And it could also mean that the dowsing students were correct in finding many of the other chakras. They just didn't dowse the ones at the extremities of the double-diamonds to find all twelve. Unravelling plant mysteries is an evolving understanding!

Plant spirit dowsing

Direct dowsing and remote scanning are also useful techniques when dowsing for plant spirits. Typically, it will be easiest to detect the big ones. A good way to try for yourself is with a friendly, mature tree. Having fixed one's mind on the subject, the dryad, one can project the sensory search up the trunk. One finds them in typical form as spherical fields, large balls of energy that are usually found in the upper third of the tree, connected into the heart or crown chakra. (Sometimes more than one is found per tree.)

Are dryads always found only there? No, they can move around the tree, especially if curious enough to take a closer look at something nearby. Or they can leave the tree altogether for a short time. When they want to be seen, they might change their form into a familiar shape that someone will recognise, which is usually human-like.

Drawing up the sap

One spring morning on my farm in Australia the author had a surprise when casually looking in the direction of a young Oak tree, planted some eight years previously. The Oak buds had been almost ready to open at that point. I could clairvoyantly see the dryad of the tree, not in its usual position, but hanging upside down on the trunk. It was making drawing movements with its 'hands'. It appeared to be coaxing the sap up the trunk, earnestly encouraging the tree's re-awakening.

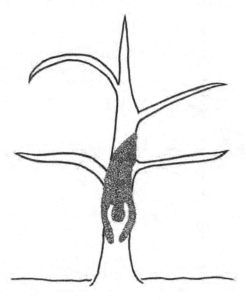

Indoor plant fairy

Is it only in a garden where you find plant spirits? Not so! The author discovered a household plant fairy in a tenth floor flat of a large concrete apartment block in Wroslaw, Poland. The resident couple had been performing Agnihotra (sacred Indian fire ceremonies) throughout the previous year there, as part of a scientific study of its effects.

As soon as I walked into the flat I felt a certain specialness in the atmosphere. The many big, beautiful indoor plants radiated health and vitality, with lots of care obviously bestowed on them. And I wasn't surprised at all when, by dowsing, I found a very contented and joyful fairy stationed on top of the largest plant. This discovery was a source of great delight for both the deva and my friends.

Dowsing sick trees

Illness and decline of plants can manifest in altered or declining energy fields. So monitoring them by dowsing can be a useful exercise. Sick trees that are growing in geopathic stress zones can have a greatly reduced general aura size. But injuries can also cause an intensification of the etheric field of a tree, as part of it's natural healing processes.

In the UK, the Devon Dowsers did some dowsing examination of tree energies, including where there had been some damage. "The tree aura appears to extend outwards from the trunk and is particularly strong where there has been some damage in the trunk itself. A stream of energy was detected from the area where a branch had been removed, the energy was a horizontal pulsating beam, similar to energy at stone columns at spiritual sites," reported Tony Heath, secretary of the group. [2]

To avoid this problem, before planting, dowse whether the spot will be energetically suitable. Preferred spots may well be related to the dowse-able grid lines in the Earth's magnetic field, such as the Curry, Hartmann and Whitman grids. However you don't need to know about these to be able to dowse for a spot that will give the plant it's best possible chance of thriving. In fact, the less cluttered your thinking is (and grids are complex), the better chance of finding these ideal planting spots.

If sick plants are in noxious locations they may be gently transplanted (give plenty of warning first) to more energetically enhancing locations. Or Earth acupuncture can be used to neutralise any geopathic effects.

Overleaf: Another Coiled Palm
affected by geopathic stress in north Queensland.

Energy enhancement by visualisation

People who enjoy practising meditation will find this a sedate way to enhance plant growth. During meditation, the visualisation of colours or energies can be mentally broadcast directly to plants. Specifically, says American dowser T. Edward Ross, one can reinforce a plant's helical spin to create perfect resonance, by such means as sound, color, electricity, light, heat, chemicals and the right mental note. Observed benefits of these practices have been unusually good soil conditions, good quality vegetable yields, and protection from insect and animal invasion.

Ross's method is simple: in deep meditation, one visualises placing a four-part helical cone over every seed, seedling and garden plot, requesting the energy cone's reinforcement and its resonance with those waveforms natural to the location and each particular variety. This needs to be done only once and it will be active until the end of the growing season, he reported. [5]

Chapter seven:
Garden dowsing

Chapter seven:
Garden dowsing

"The rod or pendulum is a read-out device of a mind state in resonance with the waveform of the cherished target." T Edward Ross

Seed dowsing and magnetising

Apart from checking plant energies, there are many other worthwhile applications of dowsing to practise in the garden. To start with, one might test seeds to find out which ones are male or female, should this be useful to know (i.e. it's best to do it as a meaningful exercise). The polarity of yang (male) or yin (female) energy in seeds can be seen in the direction of the pendulum's rotation when it's swung over them. To do this, the author would advocate first swinging the pendulum in a neutral oscillation at a distance away, then moving it over to swing above the seed. Then, asking to see the seed's yin or yang quality, you allow the pendulum's oscillations to become rotations and note which polarity these indicate.

Seed dowsing has been practised over many years in Australia, where it was popularised by the late Esther Deans in the 1980's. (Esther, along with the author and several others, helped to found the New South Wales Dowsers Society in 1984 and it is still going strong!) With her widespread promotion of natural and, in particular, no-dig gardening methods, Esther helped to bring dowsing and gardening into public view. Always keeping things simple, in her talks and book on the subject, she would refer to 'boy' and 'girl' seeds.

Another aspect of seeds that can be dowsed is checking for life-force, to gauge their level of viability. As you swing the pendulum directly over them you watch for the size and vitality of the rotations. Then you might also compare the life-force of one batch of seeds with another.

To make comparisons of viability you can also use a scale to measure with. Many dowsers use a well-known measurement system called the Bovis scale. Or if you were to ask for what percentage of seeds were viable, then your scale would be zero to one hundred. Or the use of a

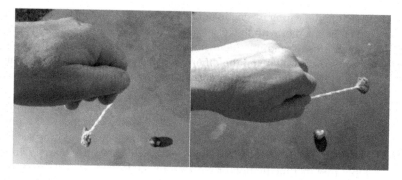

ruler can be quick and easy. As the pendulum swings over the seeds, you scan with the free hand up the ruler's length until the pendulum indicates a number by rotating. The higher the number, the more viable they are. If you are good at visualising you might simply imagine checking with a ruler; or verbalise the process by slowly counting out the numbers one to ten while your pendulum swings in neutral, until it changes to a rotation.

Seed attunement practise helps with your ongoing development of ever greater sensitivity. Eventually you may not need to use the pendulum at all. You might then simply feel directly, with your hands or other body sensors, the life-force waiting to burst out of the seeds. Your mind may start to engage in their consciousness too and the seeds will let you know that they are alive! When in springtime they sense the call for new growth and they see you as a potential agent to give them life, it must cause them to seek a connection with you. They want to be noticed and attended to! You might then share in the seeds' excitement at the prospect of being sown and living out their lives under your care and protection.

Dowsing can also be useful if you want to energetically enhance seed germination. The use of magnets has been a well attested way to achieve this. To try it yourself, you first need to check by dowsing which pole of the magnet is required, what strength of magnet is appropriate for the job and how long an exposure the seeds should be given. Magnetised water can also be used to soak seeds in. Once again, check for the correct pole and length of exposure of the magnet to the water, as well as the length of time seeds should be soaked in it. Otherwise exposure of seeds to the wrong magnetic pole could give a stunting effect! I won't equate the magnet with the terms 'north' and 'south' poles, as this can create confusion and mis-identification. It is more important to know that one pole is yang and the other has a more yin type of effect. You may find that both magnetic poles are required.

Seed energising can be done in other ways. For example, by cupping the hands around the seeds and directing life-force into them for a few minutes. I have heard of an Irish farmer who would place his crop seeds, prior to sowing them, on top of an ancient ritual stone on his farm. Other people find that meditation or blessing of seeds is ideal for promoting germination and this follows on from more ancient traditions. (There's more on such later in the book.)

One method I wouldn't waste time on has been promoted by the *Anastasia* book series and movement. They purport to convey spiritual wisdom from the Siberian wilderness. A suggestion they give is to put seeds of food plants into one's mouth before sowing them. This is supposedly to allow seed to absorb one's DNA so the plant can know what is needed to provide for our personal nutrition. (The concept is based on their premise that all nature has been created to serve humankind.) In the author's view, if soil isn't adequate for the plant, this factor will more likely dictate the nutritional value of the crop than a sliver of saliva ever can. While apparently full of well-meaning suggestions, these books are more like cult objects than practical guides for seeking harmony with nature.

Select most suitable species

There are many factors at work in any garden and by dowsing we can easily be guided to select plants that will thrive in the current conditions there. Each year weather conditions may vary, so annual plants can be selected to suit whatever is coming. Nature already knows the future pattern! Dowsing allows us to develop our innate ability to intuitively *go with the flow*.

This intuitive approach was traditional in Sri Lanka, as the author saw in a museum display there thirty years ago. By some divinatory means, farmers would check at a temple before the planting season for what crop varieties would be ideal to grow. With a reliance on monsoonal weather systems, these could sometimes fail to arrive. Or, conversely, they could bring deluges and floods. So farmers directed their prayers to discovering what was going to be the best variety to plant for the coming season. (They would have had a huge diversity of crop varieties suited to all conditions to choose from.)

One method a dowser can use is to make a list of potential candidates and to swing the pendulum over each plant name. If it stays in a neutral oscillation, then that particular plant is not going to be suitable for your situation. Only a positive rotation will indicate the best plants for the time and place.

Determine soil corrections

Soil isn't always perfectly suited to the plants you wish to grow. Soil science itself is complex, but dowsing can be a more accessible aid to ramping up soil fertility. And it can look into the more subtle influences at work as well, something a laboratory test will ignore. Is it still worth doing a lab test, to double-check? Well, possibly. The 'Weekly Times' newspaper in Victoria, Australia, several years back took a sample of topsoil that was well mixed up and divided into eighteen samples. These were sent to eighteen different testing laboratories and the same soil gave out eighteen different test results!

So you might as well try dowsing to test the soil. This way you can experiment with discovering what to apply, how often to do it and how much is needed. You can monitor the results and tweak as necessary. By dowsing, soil amendments can be selected and comparisons made between them. One can scan down the lists provided to ascertain the most beneficial soil additives. Or make up your own lists.

Then you might draw up a triangle chart on a large piece of paper to place soil and plant samples on two of the corners. (To get proper results, you must always have in mind the particular crop you want to grow in that soil.) Gather samples of the soil amendments that were indicated by dowsing the lists. These are placed on the third point for testing each in turn. You can dowse for the best quantities and times to apply them, and find out which are the best combinations of them for your designated crop. Products might be compared. For example, there may be several lime or basalt quarries in your region to choose from, so seek out which ones are going to be the best source for your soil.

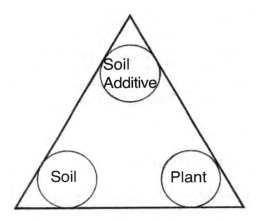

You might also dowse for the level of paramagnetism in soil, which is normally measured by how much a magnet is (weakly) attracted to it. High paramagnetism indicates a greater magnetic flux in soil, this stimulates soil microbes into action and results in enhanced fertility. Diamagnetic soils that repulse a magnet are usually considered to be of low fertility. Testing machines designed by Prof. Phil Callahan can be purchased at some expense. Or save your money and dowse it!

To raise levels of paramagnetism, the very best soil additive is crushed basalt rock, which is super rich in minerals and also raises the pH as it is very alkaline (so it can replace lime applications on acidic soils). You can also raise soil paramagnetism by increasing the amount of air in it, with digging/aerating, or better still, raised beds. Oxygen is essential for aerobic soil bacteria, while oxygen itself is highly paramagnetic.

Many other energies can impact on gardens and soil, these include energies coming from local flora and fauna, including you, your neighbours and the nature spirits too. So a general check through the lists overleaf is a good starting place.

Garden dowsing lists

Essentials for soil fertility
* soil structure (loam/clay/sand)
* minerals (replenish with rock dust)
* organic matter (carbon content, ideally above 3%)
* soil microbes (replenish with compost, worm castings)
* water (ideally free from chlorine, i.e. not tap water)
* air (oxygen, carbon dioxide))
* other

Soil and garden energies:
* cosmic - sun, moon, planets
* earth energies - noxious, beneficial
* paramagnetism - low, medium, high
* diamagnetism - low, medium, high
* flora and fauna - happy, not happy
* human - emotional, spiritual, historical
* devas - happy, not happy
* pollution - chemical, electro-smog, other
* other

Organic soil additives
* compost or worm castings
* blood & bone
* manure or urine
* fish emulsion
* seaweed
* herbs (eg comfrey, nettles)
* potash (wood ash)
* mycorrhizal fungi
* sea minerals
* Epsom salts (Magnesium sulphate)
* biochar dust / crushed charcoal
* wood chips mulch
* woody material buried
* straw/hay mulch
* other

Rock dusts
* lime
* dolomite
* gypsum
* bentonite
* zeolite
* rock phosphate
* basalt
* granite dust
* coal fines
* quartz sand
* other

Match plants with companion species

One can also dowse for ideal companion plants to group together in the garden. These can enjoy beneficial relationships with each other, while you avoid selecting plants that might be antagonistic to neighbours. Some of these relationships are already well known. For example Walnut trees are best left out of the garden as they make lousy neighbours. But other supposed good companions don't always do as well as they are said to. For example planting Marigolds with Tomatoes is supposed to deter pests. But a commercial organic farmer the author knew did a trial with these plants and found no benefit whatsoever. He felt afterwards that it might have been better to use a highly aromatic cousin of the Marigold, the Stinking Roger plant. By asking the pendulum first, one can avoid plants being mis-matched.

There can be more to this selection approach than just seeking neighbourly plants. Taking a permaculture perspective, one can also aim to create groups or 'guilds' of plants. You choose ones that are happy to grow together in terms of their similar requirements for watering, feeding, microclimate or cultivation methods. For example, you might select good neighbour wetland plants to grow together in a boggy patch; a few friendly Mediterranean herbs for a well-drained area; or a group of various root crops to grow together on top of a *Hugelkultur* mound (a raised bed that features woody material at its base, making it very fungal friendly).

Dowse for best planting location and orientation

It's worthwhile dowsing for an exact spot to best locate individual plants, especially if they are valuable or rare specimens. From an energetic viewpoint, beneficial, neutral and non-beneficial locations for plants exist everywhere. You need to avoid potentially killing precious specimens by planting them on non-beneficial energy spots. For example, many types of fruit trees will often sicken or die when planted in a geopathic zone. To avoid this, tune into the plant and ask whether it will thrive or dive in the spot you have chosen. Otherwise you can seek out the best spot for it in a given area by dowsing first.

One might do this by scanning across the subject area with the fingers and hand, while the pendulum in the other hand swings in neutral. When pointing towards a suitable spot, the oscillations will change to rotations to indicate this. If the plant is small enough, you can hold it in the scanning hand as you scan across the site, your arm acting like a directional-pointing dowsing rod, as in the photo on the right.

Dowsers speak of various universal or Earth energy grids that may influence plant growth, especially if the plant is located on strong grid lines. It's a complex subject which isn't essential to know about if you use a general approach of asking for the suitability of a location.

There is also a preferred orientation that a plant would like to grow in (and this has nothing to do with orientation to the sun). When planting, one seeks to correctly align its *critical rotational point* which, one imagines, helps the plant to connect it into Earth's electro-magnetic field at a particular phase-angle, somewhat like a key fitting properly in a lock.

To do this, (as in the photo overleaf) one first mentally attunes to the plant for a few moments. Fix your mind on what you want to achieve. Then slowly rotate the plant around through 360 degrees with one hand, while penduling with the other. Ask the plant to let you know when at it's preferred orientation.

When you have become accustomed to practising this, you might put the pendulum away and simply rotate a plant slowly around using both hands and feeling for the correct position. When reaching its preferred orientation and a positive response is elicited, plant as indicated.

For the author, at that point there is a feeling of 'stickiness', of it not wanting to turn any further around. Or I might feel a rush of energy shooting up my arms when the orientation is right.

Practising this technique whenever you can at planting time is a great exercise in plant attunement, at the very least! And plants thrive all the better for doing it. The author has used this method for many years and achieves wonderful plant growth.

Trees and the Curry Grid -
Dave Kennett's Auria Arid Region Agroforestry
Research Project, Western Australia

Dave Kennett bought degraded ex-wheat farm land with a plan to bring it back to fertility and productivity with the planting of mixed native tree species. Dave discovered that the trees he was planting at Auria would grow better if planted in preferred locations in relation to soil types and aspects of the Earth's magnetic field, as determined by dowsing. He planted many thousands of trees according to their location preferences. These went on to enjoy fantastic growth rates and high praise from visiting scientists.

"In 2001 I purchased 440acres (178 Ha) of badly neglected farmland in a semi-arid region of the Western Australian Wheatbelt. In 2008 the neighbouring 160 acres (64 Hectares) was also purchased. Of the total 600 acres (242 Ha) 50% was salt-degraded floodplain and the other 50% arable land which at best can be described as having had very low potential for agriculture. Evidently many people in the district had leased it for a few seasons with a view to purchasing it if their crops performed well, but none did.

"I did not know anything about trees when I purchased the property, nor did I know where soil types and changes occurred. Having prepared rows for planting, I would take a trailer full of trees and ask my divining rod which trees I should plant along the particular row and they were subsequently planted. My concept was to observe what survived along the rows and then plant more of them in adjacent rows at a later date.

"Now I determine the start and end point of the proposed planting row, specifying the species that I intend to plant. Here in Australia this invariably includes Eucalypts, Acacias and Melaleucas - all of which I have determined enjoy symbiotic relationships and thus enhance each other's performance. Different species of trees and shrubs have root systems that explore down to different depths. And as anyone sees when a road passes through a cutting, there are layers of different soil types.

"Now I use my iPhone with a mapping application and drive along the row and measure the distance along it where significant soil changes occur. Having done this I then determine, by divining, which trees are predisposed to the different parts of the row, the order in which they should be planted and the distances apart. The need for this all became obvious when, after growing well for seven or eight years, trees died in patches across the paddock.

"It also became obvious that other influences than soil were at work. Along any row, trees of the same type would have differing rates of growth. There is an electromagnetic grid pattern that covers every land mass known as the Curry Grid, with grid lines of energy that run NW to SE and NE to SW. It's size depends on the distance from the equator and within each grid quadrangle (they are not squares) there are 500 minor energy lines running in the same direction as the grid itself. This results in 250,000 intersection points, every one of which is akin to a different radio station.

"Each tree species/variety prefers to be 'tuned into' a particular intersection point of the Curry Grid. Any tree that snags 'the right place' will out-perform the others. Up to about 30 centimetres (1foot) from the ideal place the trees will perform reasonable well, while the remainder will be runts. About 1 metre (1 yard) due south of the ideal place for any tree, there is 'the worst place' for that species/variety. Snagging this place, no amount of effort will get it to survive in the long term."

Testimonials for Auria

"Plant establishment, survival and growth rates achieved by David at Auria are outstanding. It is indeed satisfying to see a practical application of mixed species and companion plantings across such a wide range of potentially commercially viable trees and shrubs. Any established research organisation would be proud of the successes observed in trials at Auria. The fact that they have been implemented by an individual farmer is truly remarkable." Dr David Deeley BSc, Grad Dip NRM, MSc, PhD - a Landscape Ecologist with 30 years experience.

"David defies all good forestry precepts by planting through to early summer and refusing to use chemical weed control, fertilisers or pest control. His trees have nevertheless developed astonishingly well in their first few years, even on the worst parts of the site!" Charles Peaty, BSc (Forestry) with 50 years experience.

Find best day and time to plant

Long term experiments by Maria Thun and colleagues have confirmed the ancient lore of planetary influences on plant growth. So your garden may thrive all the better if you choose cosmically ideal planting times. This can be done either by following the Thuns' biodynamic planting calendars, or you might like to try dowsing over the calendar and timepiece.

Bear in mind that biodynamic planting regimes have been developed from a regional perspective. In other parts of the world there may be other more important considerations to follow. In the authors experience of gardening in dryland Australia, best planting times were more influenced by the coming of rain, which is always such an excellent fertiliser and gives relief to heat and the often massive evaporation rates that can wither the hardiest of seedlings.

Determine if plants are affected by noxious energies

It has long been known by dowsers and foresters that plants can react quite strongly to the energies of geopathic zones, such as those caused by underground water flows or geological faults. Trees growing in these zones might develop large swellings on their trunks, sometimes called 'tree cancers'; or they may be strangely twisted; or ones that would normally have a single trunk have a second or extra trunks; or they will start to branch much closer to the ground than usual. Plants will often be stunted or lean in curious ways, or simply look stressed, or fail to thrive. This may occur in lines in a forest, with the lines following linear geopathic zones.

So gaining experience with water divining is a good practise for the developing garden dowser. It is fundamental to geomantic surveying of land and buildings as well. Much information about underground water and water divining is in the author's book 'The Wisdom of Water'. There is also a lot of information about geopathic stress in 'Divining Earth Spirit'. [1]

The great thing is that not all plants react badly to geopathic stress. Some plants just love to grow in strong energy zones, for instance Oaks, Firs, Peach and Cherry trees. However, such exposures can make them more prone to lightning strike and the Oak tree is well known for that. While such trees may 'soak up' radiations and provide us with protection to some degree, they may also suffer ill-effects in the long run.

If might be worthwhile checking the garden for electro-smog too. You will need to buy or borrow a meter for magnetic fields (a gaussmeter) and a high-frequency meter for microwave and radiowave detection, as seen on the right. (Not all frequencies are picked up by all meters, however. So, if in doubt - dowse!) If there are waves of toxic radiation beaming from a particular direction, such as from a mobile phone tower or military base, you might be able to plant a 'sacrifice crop' of fast growing vegetation in that direction, to act as an energetic screen and, when dense or tall enough, make the garden safer to be in. For example, Eucalyptus trees are known for their ability to screen out electro-smog.

Above: Checking for high frequency electro-smog. Ideally it's below ten microwatts per square metre. For the electro-sensitive author, below one (as above) is much better!

By checking the garden for any noxious energies, ideally before planting it out, one can either avoid planting there or design around harnessing geopathic energies for enhanced plant growth. This is a sound permaculture design approach, with site energies initially assessed and then made the best possible use of. For example, in Germany where geopathic stress is found in the garden it is traditional to plant Box trees. These are popular garden plants used for hedging and topiary work. But if plants are already growing in a bad position and not happy? You could always dig them up and re-plant them in a more benign spot, to give them a new start in life, as the following story shows.

Moscow's sick street trees
- Dowser to the rescue!

Moscows street trees have a hard time surviving the grime, air pollution, and the salt and chemicals from snow clean ups etc. By the early 1990's an estimated 70% were sick and dying. Well known dowser Alex Dubrov discovered that the trees that succumbed first to stresses were additionally under geopathic stress, including Hartmann grid energy.

After much lobbying, eventually the city officials used his information in a five year trial starting in 1997-98, and they are now doing follow up. As a result of the affected trees being re-positioned away from geopathic and other stress zones, some 80% of them are now healthy and thriving, Sergey Bondarchuk (president of the Russian Scientific Dowsing Society) informed us at the International Dowsing Congress held in Manchester, UK, in September 2003.

Determine if soil is polluted

Is your soil contaminated? Do plants keel over in it? Perhaps you live in an ex-mining area and it had toxic waste dumped here and there. This was the case in the Goldfields region of Victoria, Australia, where the author used to live. Local horses sometimes died from eating grass on soil that was an alarming purple colour. It had been poisoned by gold mining chemicals dumped on it well over a century ago.

It's good to also check for any history of pesticide use, such as in banana growing regions where DDT is a highly persistent soil toxin, breaking down into toxic daughter products and lingering on for who-knows-how-long. It's not always possible to see evidence of such toxicity.

For a laboratory analysis you need to know what to have soil checked for. Dowsing could save time and money, by asking if the area or soil is best avoided, or in need of remedial action. You might be able to give it a de-tox using special mushrooms or microbes, or grow a sacrifice crop such as celery that is disposed of accordingly. (Celery is very good at taking up heavy metals!)

Determine plant healing methods

Techniques of plant healing might be selected by dowsing. Often the energetic remedies used for humans and animals will work just as well on plants. For example, for human shock the classic vibrational remedy of Bach Flowers - *Rescue Remedy* - can work wonders. A plant being transplanted can be helped by spraying it with water to which a few drops of Rescue Remedy has been added, as in the photo.

Hands on healing methods, such as Reiki, can also be applied to sick plants. And a regular pep talk to them can do wonders too! In 'Stone Age Farming' the use of copper coils was discussed. These are all designed according to dowsing.

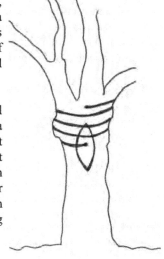

As an example, for a simple healing coil one checks for the appropriate end of a length of copper wire (i.e. correct polarity) and attaches this end to the front door/heart chakra on the plant stem (as on the right). It is then wound up the stem for a dowsed number of rings (none of which should be touching each other), spiralling either clockwise or anti-clockwise.

Geomantic garden design

Where to begin with a plant-spirit-friendly approach to gardening? How to navigate amongst the fairies? It's usually best to start with discovering the energies of place. All energy flows, points and fields of any significance (including the hot spots for devas) can be found by dowsing and recorded on a garden plan. (If you lack confidence, get someone else to do it for you.) You can then go on to design around any strong energies by avoiding, harnessing or honouring them.

A garden energy survey might indicate a need to re-balance or cleanse the energetic landscape. In this case the chart provided (page 143) may be useful to determine which techniques might be best to try out. To correct any dis-harmony, one can dowse for the best spot for an earth acupuncture treatment, or an attractive stone arrangement; select appropriate types of stone and the like. This requires some proficiency with dowsing. But if unsure, it's worth trying and one can monitor the effects and tweek later, if necessary.

Some dowsers create lovely garden beds by dowsing for the best site, or by linking them in with natural energy flows. Pathways might be made to follow energetic flows and the shape of a garden bed can also be determined by dowsing. Use your intuition!

Above: Curving pathways wind through delightful gardens at the Organic Centre, North Leitrim, Ireland.

Following the principles of feng shui, one ideally incorporates curving designs wherever possible. This encourages beneficial ch'i to accumulate. With paths and waterways thus curvily meandering, one plants on the edges. This gives plants the benefit of *edge effect*, giving them extra light, rain, air, helpful bugs and your attention.

Another approach is to erect a *Tower of Power*, also called a Paramagnetic Antenna. This acts as a wave-guide that collects solar magnetism, intensifying magnetic field strength in the area around it and thus enlivening soil microbes and stimulating plants and animals. A Tower can be made from a plastic pipe filled with paramagnetic basalt stone dust and positioned over a downward geo-spiral (vortex). Ideally you locate the garden close by or around it, so that plants can benefit from the most concentrated part of the energy field. Power Towers put such a stimulating energy into the garden, it may be too much for some people if located close to the home. So check that the extra energy from an envisioned Tower is also going to be okay for people. For more details, read the author's book 'Stone Age Farming'. [2]

Left: Feeling the energy of a newly made Power Tower, in Bavaria, Germany, May 2016.

Garden Energy Harmonising and Enhancement Dowsing List

Earth Acupuncture

metal stakes, special stones, amethyst crystal, copper coils, selected plants and colours, Tower of Power

Stone Arrangements

labyrinth, stone circle, standing stone, medicine wheel, paramagnetic or diamagnetic rock

Symbolic Patterns

yantra, circle, geometric shape, mandala, word or glyph, Reiki symbol

Landscape Features

altar, spirit house, special tree / grove/ plant, garden mound, pond, sculpture, artwork, waterway, pyramid, wilderness zone

Other

Above: Copper pyramid on wooden stepped base, in a garden in Lorsch, Germany.

Determine best harvesting techniques, amounts and times

The culture of domesticated food plants goes back over ten thousand years. Traditions developed to ritualise the ideal ways to plant, tend and reap crops. There are ideal methods of sowing and harvesting that are worth knowing. Certain ways of picking produce can prolong the life of the crop and keep plants happy, and each plant will have different requirements.

Examples include picking leaves from the outside of the plant and leaving the central growing tip, so that it can go on producing new leaves. To continually nip off flower buds from plants, such as Basil, in order to lengthen their life span. And to not harvest too much from perennial plants, so they can regenerate, express themselves fully and live on. If in doubt, you might 'interview' the plant directly, with questioning by dowsing to discover how best to harvest it.

Select best locations for *earthing*

One of the personal benefits of spending time in your garden can be that it gets you well *grounded*, or *earthed*. This involves receiving a healthy flow of electrons that rise up from out of the ground to benefit you; as well as the dumping of excess, harmful electrical voltage that builds up in your body systems from static electricity and other electro-smog. Earthing can have marvellous healing effects for people and there is a huge need for it in this techno-crazy world. Thirty minutes daily grounding is recommended. [3]

But it can't happen if you wear plastic-soled shoes or socks, as these are insulators. One needs to be barefoot at the right kind of place to enjoy the benefits of earthing. Ideally your feet are on bare rock or soil, or even concrete. These are conductive materials. If you are trying to earth on a dry grass lawn, it may be futile. However, by giving the spot a soak of water beforehand, it will become more conductive. You might also consider avoiding earthing around any underground cables or where stray electrical fields could affect you.

Why not create a special place in the garden for a regular earthing routine? Dowsing for a location for your designated earthing spot that is free of any energetic hazards is a good start. Ideally the spot will be multi-functional too - a pleasant place to take rest or refreshment, with a comfortable chair and table. An all-weather location is perfect. It could be a dedicated spot in the shadehouse or hot house, wherever there's a comfortable micro-climate for the season.

Surrounded by beautiful growing plants with vibrant coloured flowers, breathing in the fresh oxygen and negative ions, and listening to bird song and insect buzz, can make the earthing routine a most wonderful time of the day in your backyard paradise. The enjoyment of watching the fruits of your labours developing means that the gardener's rewards are not just at harvest time, but continual.

And by paying attention to re-balancing your personal energies, you nurture the garden of your own self.

Garden Dowsing Applications Summary

1. Test seeds and magnetise them

2. Select species most suited to your garden

3. Determine soil correction

4. Match plants with companion species

5. Find best planting location and orientation

6. Find best day and time to plant

7. Determine if plants are affected by noxious energies

8. Determine if soil is polluted

9. Determine plant healing methods

10. Design energised and geomantically harmonised gardens

11. Determine best harvesting techniques, amounts and times

12. Select best locations for earthing

Chapter eight
Gardening with the devas

Chapter eight
Gardening with the devas

"The fairies are happy to work with us, to cooperate in making a spot of loveliness for mutual enjoyment. If only more human beings knew how eager the fairy kingdom is to help, gardens would be even more like fragments of Heaven on Earth than they are now for most of us."

Dora van Gelder.

Where can garden devas be found?

Devic life is everywhere, but it is the more evolved type of deva that is of most interest to the gardener. Fairies and other beings that love to tend the various plants under their charge have a preference for gardens that are not too tidy. If you are looking for the devas' homes, they are usually found in wild, uncultivated corners, where vegetation is lush. If you don't have such a wild corner, one can be created for their sanctuary, for deva habitat. This was done in classical Greece, where people assigned a corner of their gardens as a wild, sacred temenos.

Devas can be highly territorial beings with strong bonds of attachment to their habitat. Certain rocks and topographic features can become very important to them for various reasons. Plants provide homes and meeting places for them too. "Of course they wouldn't like you to touch a bush that would belong to them. They might want it for shelter, or it might only be because it belongs to them," an informant of Lady Gregory's told her a century ago. [1] Incurring the wrath of the devas was always warned of, as it might cause retaliation and misfortune. So keeping on their good side was, and is, always the go.

To develop a deva-friendly garden, it's important to determine which are the devas' favourite plants and places, as well as the locations of their homes and pathways, and to actively protect them. Ideally starting off with a good geomantic survey of all such elements, then, working with the energies of place, you will be well on the way to creating a fairy haven. It's best if the gardener is the one to do this as they know the place the best. Dowsing techniques are easily learned and practised, the gardener is empowered and the garden powered up too.

What do devas think of us?

Generally speaking, the devic kingdoms most associated with humankind have looked up to us with both fondness and awe. Because of their admiration, they tend to emulate human looks and fashions of the time in their astral outfits. But this relationship in the Western world mostly ended by the Middle Ages, which is why they often appear to clairvoyants and in book illustrations decked out in medieval garb.

Nowadays devas are not accustomed to being recognised, let alone honoured, and they are usually either indifferent or in dread of humans and their nature destroying activities.

It is the garden fairies that have the most affection for humans, in comparison to beings of wilder parts. Apart from the strong feelings they have for plants under their care, they often have great love for us gardeners, for young children and animals. As van Gelder notes -

"A human being who keeps a fine garden, loves and cares for his trees and plants, and perhaps even has some feelings for the plants' inner life, will attract many more of the Little People than another person may do who is indifferent to this aspect." [2]

By being a dedicated plant lover and carer, devas will greatly respect you. They may even be happy to work with you. Another way to earn the devas' admiration is by admiring 'their' works. Always smell the roses, whenever you can!

Fairies, flowers and tree connections

by Kate Twomey, flower essence practitioner,
Queensland, Australia.

"Specific areas of my garden have fairies. They are extraordinarily helpful in maintaining the environment. Initially I made flower essences from my garden and then in bushland, and chose the flower via dowsing. It is always a very reverent experience and a sheer delight to talk to the plants in this way. The last essence I made was using a ground orchid that had never appeared in that particular area before. It was a plant that has a strong micro-fungal reliance upon the larger healing trees in the area. From that essence making I learnt to 'see' the energy under the ground and that way could trace it back to the Grandmother Tree in the area."

Cut flowers and displaced devas

What do garden fairies think of us picking 'their' flowers? On this subject, Hodson reported that they are "conscious and appreciative of the admiration of human beings for their work; but, on our approach they seem to plead that the flower shall not be injured. If it is cut they will follow it into the room and stay with it for some time."

The author experienced this first hand. Having grown a magnificent specimen of Western Australian Banksia tree, I was intent to bring some of the big blooms indoors to admire. This I did and later that day, with the flowers nearby, my meditation was marred by the observation of a couple of distressed nature spirits whizzing around the room above me.

No doubt they were displaced flower fairies. I apologised to them and asked them to come with me back outdoors. I held out a small piece of Banksia branch and they attached themselves to it. We walked slowly back to their tree (seen right) and they were very happy to get back to their domain. Since then, I rarely pick flowers! If I do, I warn flower fairies first and allow them time to move away from the flowers I want to pick.

Flower blues

Flowers and their fairies have worse to suffer. On commercial flower farms the amount of chemicals they are drenched with is enormous. The author saw workers in a Malaysian flower factory, where fewer chemicals were being used than usual, packaging Chrysanthenum flowers for export. They wore face masks, because, I was told, nasal cancer is common in this industry. The flowers were, ironically, being grown for the Japanese temple trade.

Environmental destruction evident in this flower growing, central highlands region of mainland Malaysia was extreme, with jungle clad mountain sides carved out ad hoc and problems of mass erosion, landslides and flooding a consequence. It made me feel sick to see it! I pointed out to the farmers the presence of an angry landscape deva on one of the last still-forested mountain tops close by. It's form I perceived as a huge Orang Utan (a hairy primate species, once 'king of the jungle' around here). The deva was, not surprisingly, highly agitated and anxious to get its angst across to us! It's home may well be bulldozed by the neighbouring farmers by now.

Co-creating with the devas

These days many people are starting to practice co-creative gardening, based on the idea that devas and people can make a wonderful team effort together, if devic assistance is consciously invoked. This idea has been evolving since miracles of plant growth began to manifest in a garden at Findhorn, Scotland in the 1960's. Despite a harsh environment there, amazing plant growth was achieved by opening lines of communication with the consciousness of the over-lighting spirits of the food plants and gaining their advice. The ancient plant-people spiritual connection was being revived.

More recently Machaelle Small-Wright of the Perelandra Garden in the USA has inspired a new generation of co-creative gardeners to follow suit. At Perelandra, Small-Wright developed a ritual mechanism of devic communication using a form of muscle testing (equivalent to deviceless dowsing) to gain access to devic consciousness. This formalized their exchanges and enabled her to work under devic guidance.

The Perelandra method begins by saying out loud: "I wish to be formally linked with the devic realm." As contact is made one might then feel sensations, like waves of energy gently washing over you. With a divining tool, Small-Wright then asks for devic guidance in garden design, advice on what to plant and where, and how to best deal with insects. To control insect pests she offers to tithe a certain part of her crop to them. This keeps everyone happy.

The Perelandra method of fertilizing the garden also involves devas and is reminiscent of homeopathic medicine. One makes up a soil balancing kit of various organic substances suggested by the devas. This will be a collection of small packages that might include bone meal, rock phosphate, dolomite, lime, Kelp, Comfrey and the like. One then takes a pinch of each substance individually, holding it in the palm of the hand and asking the appropriate devas what amount is needed. Then one asks that they receive the energy of that nutrient and that the right amount is taken down to the right soil depth wherever it's needed in the garden. After about ten seconds the transfer is completed and it can be sensed as a change in the nutrient, or as a sensation in the hand, then the sample is thrown away, Small-Wright says.

The Perelandra garden has an incredible rate of production and is drought proof, being only watered at planting time. Small-Wright wrote that, "The devas seek a co-creative partnership with humans and they are in the position to accept no less." [3]

One doesn't have to be specially gifted to emulate this approach. Particular formulas are not absolutely necessary, but may be useful to get you going. You start with a desire for a sincere connection to the devic world. Then, by dowsing, you might locate garden devas who could be helpful and approach them gently. Pose questions to them by dowsing for yes/no answers. Or ask willing devas to come forward to assist you and be open to receiving their communications on a telepathic level. This might involve verbalising out loud what is intended to be done in the garden.

Sometimes the author will invite particular devas to visit and consult with at a certain time and place, making an appointment with them, so to speak, to give them time to come forward. An initial short period of meditation is beneficial for getting onto a resonant wavelength before connecting with them. And daily meditation keeps one's sensitivity and intuition primed for this type of work.

Biodynamic garden fairy

Garden fairies often get a great thrill from receiving recognition from people, the author finds. For example, in a beautiful biodynamic herb garden (seen overleaf) at Lindenhof near Darmstadt, Germany, a presiding deva was discovered by the author in September 2014 and revisited in June 2016. As she was so friendly, I invited this chief garden fairy to be present to meet a group of students the following day. Sure enough, at the alloted time next day, she was waiting there for us at the back of the garden. Most of the students were able to dowse her spherical devic field from a short distance away, by the remote scanning method. (It would otherwise disturb such a being, if we were too close.) She then rose up a metre or more into the air and graciously hovered around for a short time. I tracked her sideways movement, providing a running commentary. She seemed to be getting a real thrill from all the attention and was actually 'showing off' to us!

Luther Burbank's plant magic

Sensitive gardeners know that plants respond to our thoughts, feelings and intentions. Plants will glow with health and produce better when we think of them lovingly and talk to them sweetly. By resonating with love among our plants, gardening can be truly soul-satisfying work. And for the food plants that we usually take for granted, it has been a completely transformative experience of co-evolution, because most of them bear little resemblence to their wild forebears that ancient farmers bred them from.

The ancestors of our food plants were very different beasts, often unpalatable, tiny and bitter or tasteless, or even toxic. They did not want anything to digest them. Beans are well known for their anti-digestive factors, but, at the dawn of agriculture, they were far worse. Fruits and vegetables were mostly so full of defensive mechanisms that, if not outright unsuitable for consumption, they needed extensive processing to remove toxic factors and become edible.

What was achieved in terms of breeding out such defensive characteristics to make the delicious crop foods of today seems miraculous. Varieties were developed to have fewer protective mechanisms and delicious flavours. Somehow, a deal was struck in return for the harvest of crops which are often defenceless against pests, that we would propagate, nourish and protect them as they grew. How was this transformation possible? Without men in white coats and test tubes? It seems that our thoughts and feelings could be the crucial key to understanding the ancient mystery of plant breeding miracles.

Luther Burbank (1849-1926) was a legendary plant breeder in America who was able to achieve phenomenal results that can only be understood if the power of love and the intelligence of nature is properly appreciated. Burbank left the world a mind boggling legacy of eight hundred new cultivars and plant varieties that have global popularity, including the Plumcot (a Plum and Apricot cross), the Shasta daisy, Burbank potato, Freestone Peach and Santa Rosa plum, all bred over a fifty five year career.

Burbank's technique was kept mostly to himself for fear of ridicule. It seems that he was able to gain the co-operation of his plants by talking affectionately to them, lovingly suggesting how he would like them to change certain characteristics. And thus he was able to create, in some cases, tasty fruits from what had been inedible wild ones. Burbank even talked the spines off a Prickly Pear Cactus! "You don't need your defensive thorns", he would say to his thorny cactii, "I will protect you". With this repeated mantra of promising the cactus his protection, he eventually bred a spineless one and that variety is still widely grown for cattle feed to this day.

Burbank's hardy and prolific Burbank potato is also immensely popular, with a natural variant, the 'Russet Burbank', now the world's most popular variety for commercial processing. He bred the also popular Calla Lily from a graceful wild plant that had an ugly odour. From amidst 5,000 young Calla Lilies that were reared, he was able to sniff out a single specimen to breed from - it alone had a lovely fragrance.

Burbank was a mysterious character, obviously highly intuitive, who quietly attributed his success to the loving encouragement he gave his plants. This was in the form of thought transference using mental images and loving feelings. When he talked to his plants, it was "to create a vibration of love". He would envision the form that he wanted the plant to take and, showering affection on it, went on to develop new strains with the plant's full co-operation. Manly P Hall reported that "when Burbank wanted something special from a plant, he would take it into his confidence and explain exactly what peculiar and uncommon characteristics he would like the plant to develop.... Burbank believed that plants had twenty distinct senses...(and) could comprehend the meaning of his dialogue with them."

Burbank said that "the environment is the architect of evolution". And so he provided the perfect environment for his plants to achieve evolutionary fast tracking. But local people in the Santa Barbara area of California where he lived also believed Burbank to have special powers. Following the big 1906 earthquake much of Santa Rosa was destroyed. But not a single pane of glass in his glasshouses was damaged, while the main farm building was wrecked. And at a nearby photographic studio almost all of the glass plates were destroyed, with the exception of those ones of Burbank and his plant creations.

There has been a replication of Burbank's work too. A Chinese gardener inspired by him was also able to get brilliant results. So Luther Burbank is a shining example of how the power of love can potentially make plants fabulously productive or more useful to humankind and anyone who tries using this approach may well reap great rewards. [4]

Being a friend to your plants

Being friends with your plants is an ongoing process. First you earn their respect and communicate lovingly with them, showering them with affection. After you start to feel accepted and loved back, you might ask for their advice and assistance. Thank them for their help.

Before any changes are made in the garden, do a 'check-in' and consult the local devas if it's okay with them. Give plenty of advance warning to plants before removing or cutting anything. Warn of pruning, picking flowers, cutting living plants down, etc. If the devas are opposed to the plan, negotiate with them! Come to a compromise, make a deal.

Horizontal branches of trees are especially popular with the devas, often favoured by Air spirits, who like to perch on them just like birds! So check with the devas before lopping significant branches. Before you do any lopping, give the tree as much warning as you can. Then warn it a day or so before and just ahead of the event, as well. You might tie a ribbon around a limb, at the point where you intend to lop it. Trees have been observed to withdraw their sap and life energies in readiness, as a result of doing this.

Tane, god of New Zealands' forests

For the Māori people of New Zealand, abundant forests provided them with food, shelter and resources. They were vital for life. In Maori tradition, forests were also the domain of Tāne, a deity of supreme importance. Tāne separated Earth and Sky and brought the vegetated world into being. He made the first human; he adorned the Heavens and he brought the baskets of knowledge, wisdom and understanding down from the Sky to benefit humans.

Tāne has different names to reflect these roles. He is called Tāne-mahuta as god of the forest, Tāne-te-wānanga as the bringer of knowledge, and Tānenui-a-rangi as bringer of higher consciousness. To appease Tāne before felling a tree (- slaying his child), the Maori traditionally perform a special ceremony of placation. [5]

Keep fairy homes and pathways free from interference

Here and there in the garden nature spirits will have their residences. The entrances to some are often portals to underground 'tunnels' and 'caverns' (which are not necessarily of a physical nature). Locations might be a significant landscape feature. Or they may have nothing visible to distinguish them, only that they are a strong Earth energy point, such as where energy flows are crossing. Accounts of clairvoyants describe the appearance of some of the devas' homes as small models of human houses made from astral matter. Near the author's home in

Ireland, for example, a family of *cluricauns* (rather cheeky little Earth elemental beings) live in a tiny replica of a clay-straw timber studio, not far from the real thing! So identify the homes of fairies and the like and avoid any unwanted developments in their near vicinity.

Where the devas travel along *Fairy Lines* is also very important to keep clear. Interfering with them is a well known no-no in Irish tradition. Many a 'fairy story' warns of the consequences to the family and their animals. Sometimes a house was built with a corner deliberately cut off, to avoid it cutting through a Fairy Path and asking for trouble. The old Irish cottages that defied ancient wisdom and were built across Fairy Lines would have a lot of visitors travelling through them in the other dimensions. There might be mysterious nightly openings of locked doors or annoyed presences felt. When the already mentioned studio building was about to be built across a Fairy Pathway, the author had a season of negotiating with the local fairy queen and the pathway had to be diverted. Now all is good!

What is the nature of a Fairy Pathway exactly? It is a type of energy flow that emerges from the ground in an upward spiralling geo-vortex. It then flows along the contours of the landscape in a curving serpentine form, following the same laws of movement as in fluid dynamics. Larger versions have been traditionally called *Dragon Lines* (*lung mei*) in Chinese geomancy. But from the shape of them one might better describe them as 'Serpent Lines'. The devas find these energy flows convenient to travel allow, although they are not restricted to them and can move wherever they wish.

When a Fairy Line goes back down into the Earth at a downward geo-vortex, it might be called in Ireland a *Fairy Hole*. This can be a fairy home and the author has just such a geo-vortex fairy home in a field in Ireland. It has been protected by encircling it with a ring of stones and Oak trees to create a place that can be sacred to all beings.

Plant green ribbons, sacred trees and Deva Stations

Devas will be most impressed if you plant a wild meadow with native plants, or designate a temenos, a wilderness zone for their safe sanctuary. Planting 'green ribbons' of vegetation to connect up isolated green areas will also benefit the devas. Wildlife will be able to move around more extensively and this is good for genetic biodiversity. Continuous green belts or hedgerows are perfect for *Connecting Country* (a term which also happens to be a fabulous Landcare intitiative in Australia).

Below: Hedgerow field boundaries criss-cross the Irish countryside and provide a wild zone in the rural landscape where trees might otherwise be few.

Planting a sacred tree or grove is a great thing to do and it can also provide multiple benefits, from a permaculture viewpoint, when carefully placed in the landscape. Richard Webb of Permaculture Asia Ltd. in Hong Kong studied the tradition and environmental significance of sacred Chinese feng shui groves. These forest remnants are usually found in significant locations where they are fundamental in helping prevent soil erosion in the water catchment, slowing down the movement of wind and water, and thus increasing the comfort and protection of people, livestock and crops. They also provide a refuge for wildlife and nature spirits, Webb discovered.

Designated wilderness zones, an important component of permaculture design, likewise can protect remnant vegetation and provide undisturbed water catchment areas. They can help maintain biodiversity for all the kingdoms of nature. Known as *Zone Five* in permaculture design, some people might call them *Deva Stations*, although the stations of the devas can also be individual landscape features that they like to attach to, or visit on their territorial rounds.

Your wild temenos area can be made sacred for you as well, if it includes a place for meditation and contemplation. While leaving it undisturbed mostly, one can also harvest various products such as honey from bees, mushrooms and tree seeds. It need not be 'unproductive'.

To create a woodland in your Zone Five area, natural forest regeneration could be allowed for minimal effort. By keeping out stock and controlling weeds initially, seeds will blow in and trees will appear with increasing biodiversity over time. Or sow seeds directly on site. Apart from a bit of thinning if saplings are overcrowded there should not be too much work to do. Once seedlings are up thickly and shading the ground, competition is suppressed. No more weeding! If planting a woodland with saplings, try to source the local genotypes, plants that are endemic to the area and thus perfectly suited to the growing conditions.

You might also find out what native trees in your area have sacred associations, to include them in a sacred grove and not upset the balance of an existing flora/fauna/deva community. To illustrate this point, in central Australia some of the local sacred tree species are the River Red Gum (Eucalyptus teretecornis) and Emu Bush (Eremophila longifolia). I heard of a reafforestation project in that region where it was intended to plant Eucalypts from another area to stabilise a riverbank. But when the local Aboriginal people were consulted one woman was not happy with the plan. She was emphatic that this was not a good idea as it would "confuse the Dreaming" of the land, by using a non-local species.

The Dreaming is a loosely descriptive English term for an Australian Aboriginal concept of the other-dimensional worlds of country and nature, in other words - the *geomancy* of place. Mythic Dreamtime creation stories have been passed down through the generations for around fifty thousand years, in the world's oldest continuing culture. This is the first time that the author has seen a *geomantic* reason given for being a *Bush Regeneration* purist and maintaining the original endemic plant species mix at a site. But it hasn't been the last time, so it is a point worth considering when planning a woodland. Often you will find that the function of a tree that you are needing can be found in a local species. So work out what outcomes you want from your woodland before selecting species and ideally keep it local and natural.

Maintain only good thoughts in the garden

Devas find the energy of most humans rather abhorrent. But they do seem to love little children and they can often be detected at playgrounds, especially where children are happily playing, as they delight in watching and being around them. If you make your garden a joyful place, you are more likely to attract devas to live there. And that's good for you too, because the garden can be your best place to relax, play and unwind, as well as get fit and healthy.

Places to sit, slow down and contemplate nature are a must. You might make a special place to meditate and ground yourself, or find a magic spot for saying thanks to *them*. A seat with some stone paving, or a bench or a pile of straw could be the go for getting focussed on happy thoughts. The devas will love that! Only go into the garden when you have happy thoughts and feelings. Stay away if you're in a bad mood! Or else you might negatively affect the environment. There are old tales of plants withering under the perishing gaze of a show-off shaman or magician.

On the other hand, by positively harnessing mind power in the garden, people can generate wonderfully beneficial results. Focussed meditation directed at seeds and amongst crop plants in India is a key technique in *Sustainable Yogic Agriculture*, or SYA (called Pranic Agriculture in the USA). A modern movement that is derived from India's ancient wisdom, it is starting to be practised world-wide these days.

The SYA initiative involves around 400 farmers from central and northern India who are enjoying improved, sustainable outcomes. It all began after farmer Nanu Ram, a regular meditator, found his crops suffering greatly from pests and so he started to experiment with focussed meditation to stop them. He meditated on this thought –

> *"The vegetation is filled with light and might, and the insects are weak and no longer welcome. They should be gone."*

After a couple of hours of meditation over two or three days the insect population of Nanu Ram's experimental crop was noticeably less. Ram shared his findings at the local Brahma Kumaris centre and the news quickly spread amongst local farming families. Thus, the *Yogic Kheti Agriculture* initiative, as the Indians call it, was born in 2009.

SYA is described as a systematic thought-based meditation that's practised at all stages of the crop cycle, with methods of traditional organic farming also bringing benefit. Meditation is practiced on seeds, then at sowing, watering and harvesting times, both remotely and in the field. The meditators focus thoughts of peace, non-violence, love, strength and resilience on the seeds for up to a month before sowing them. Seeds that have been meditated upon germinate much quicker than regular seeds, at around one week earlier.

The effectiveness of SYA has been studied and documented by a co-operative of scientists from leading Indian agricultural universities. The scientists have noted that: "In the yogic farm fields there are greater quantities of Rhizobium, Azotobacter, Azospirillium and PSB (phosphate solubilizing bacteria) - indicating improved soil health". The scientists also found that seeds and crops have elevated levels of iron, energy, protein and vitamins compared to control plots of chemically farmed and organic grown food. Farmers using SYA methods are saving much money from the elimination of chemical costs. There are less farmer suicides now and farmer health and wellbeing is much improved.

A farmer's wife from one of the SYA villages summed it up when saying that - "There is no doubt that our family is healthier now. You can definitely taste the difference in the food. Also, my husband is no longer getting sick from pesticides." [6]

Negative thoughtforms

Mind techniques are valuable, but one must also be warned that negative thinking can be very powerful too. This is why Irish Blessing Stones, still found in a few old churchyards, are also known as Cursing Stones, because they were magical focussing devices that could be used for both. (Traditionally the act of cursing was only done against some injustice, such as when peoples' land was stolen from them. If it was unjustified, one could expect a backlash!) The smooth rounded stones on their flagstone tables (such as the one below, in an old churchyard in County Roscommon) were ritually turned clockwise for blessing and anti-clockwise to curse, while prayers were uttered. And yes, they can and do work. Otherwise they would not still be here today! [7]

Some people use mental techniques to banish plant predators. But it's probably not a good idea to broadcast 'bad', combative or angry thoughts towards them. It could increase any general negativity and taint the feng shui. For example, yelling at your chickens at regular intervals for scratching the garden (which is perfectly natural behaviour for them) will affect the emotional aura of the land. The devas won't like it either.

A better approach is to send positive, loving energy to plants and to mentally encourage them to have greater resilience against pests, as the pranic farmers do. Talk kindly to the pests and negotiate with them about which of your plants you are happy for them to eat and which ones are only for you. And keep chickens out of the garden with good fencing!

Keep fairy areas toxin and metal free

In tradition, fairies own the wild places, unworked by the plough. This could partly be because the plough is iron, which is anathema to them (as is the chemicals used by gardeners and farmers). T C Lethbridge, an English researcher in the early part of the 20th century, used dowsing for much of his investigations into the other-dimensional realities. His studies of subtle energies found what others have long known, that "metal interrupts energy". This is why the fairies have traditionally abhorred iron.

Earth energy flows can be broken by metal fences or sheds that cross them. Ideally, a fairy-friendly garden has the barest minimum of metal in it, of iron and steel that is. Even parking your bicycle or wheelbarrow on a Fairy Path is asking for trouble! You may also want to replace some of your gardening tools with wooden or bronze versions, as they are energetically better for the soil and also 'fairy-approved'.

New Bronze Age

When teaching people about dowsing in the garden in Europe a common question to the author has been: "What about slugs?!" They are the bane of the gardeners life! While some people consider slugs to be nature's little helpers in cleaning up ageing and sick plants, which is true, they are also partial to devouring newly transplanted vegetables and are hard to exclude from the garden.

So when buying a set of bronze garden tools the author was delighted to read that, as well as helping to maintain energetic harmony in the garden, they might also repel slugs. It was early springtime and slugs were starting to appear. And though pots of tasty young plants were now in their sights, there was virtually no slug damage!

This was assisted by the presence of bands of copper impregnated material that are wrapped around my Bucket Gardens (which are 15 litre buckets made of food grade plastic, that function as portable *Wicking*

Gardens, having a water reservoir in the bottom of them, as below.) Slugs can't handle copper, on making contact it gives them a shock. But when the copper bands get dirty they become ineffective. I had just given my buckets a spring clean, refreshing the compost, sand and soil mix in them and scrubbing the anti-slug collars clean before planting them out with vegetable seedlings.

My new bronze tools had arrived and they were a delight to use. The 'fairy-friendly' tools, handmade by PKS in Austria and Hungary, have blades of solid bronze, which is an alloy of copper and tin. They never rust, have sharp edges that are hard wearing and stay sharp, and they slide easily into the soil. The whole feel of using them is different! Inspired by the work of Austrian maverick Victor Schauberger, PKS was established by his family to preserve and promote his work.

Why copper? PKS explains that "in many ways, copper is the opposite of iron and steel, the metals commonly used for garden tools. Iron is magnetic, copper is conductive. So, whereas iron tools can disturb the soil magnetism, copper assists the flow of Earth energies to nourish the plants. Iron is a base metal, so it rusts when exposed to air. Copper (along with silver and gold) is a noble metal, which does not corrode easily. This means it leaves less of a residue in the soil.

"Slugs and snails have no natural magnetism - literally. Their blood is based on copper, whereas we have iron flowing in our veins. Iron is magnetic, while copper is non-magnetic and highly conductive. This has significance for gardeners, as many users of our garden tools have found out. This quality of their blood means that slugs and snails do not seem to be attracted to plants cultivated with our tools.

"As long as the bronze tool is the last one to touch the soil before leaving the transplanted seedlings, it offers some protection while the young plants establish themselves. It's not completely mollusc-proof - we still notice some slug and snail damage in our garden. But nothing like the complete devastation of young plants that we used to experience," the company stated. [8]

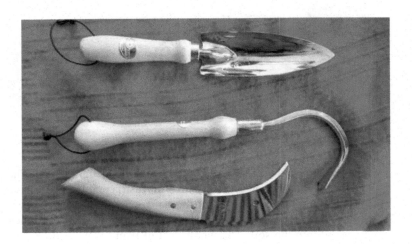

Re-locate plant devas if necessary

German tree spirit Miller told of how he liked to sometimes leave his home and go off with his human friends for short outings. [9] The author once toured the garden in such a way, with a Carob tree dryad in tow to help me in selecting the best spots for new Carob trees. It helped me to locate them just above the frost line and so subsequently, none were damaged by frost.

Dryads can also transfer themselves from a fallen tree, moving home into a young tree nearby to take charge of its welfare. So if you have to remove a plant, or if a tree has blown down in a storm, you might invite the displaced deva to attach itself temporarily onto a piece of *live wood*, such as one of its twigs, that you hold out to it. Ask it to come with you to a new home, a new replacement plant/tree that will be planted or is existent (having checked suitability first). Advance warnings and apologies must be profusely given, of course.

When you feel that the deva is ready and has attached itself to the twig, walk very slowly, holding the wood deferentially, and you might feel its energy moving with your own. Talk to it frequently, tell it what is happening, give it encouragement to move on. When you arrive and place the twig onto the new plant, tell the plant spirit to go into its new home and let it know that it will always be safe there under your loving protection.

Gardening with the Devas Summary

1.   Be a good friend to your plants

2.   Consult the local devas before any changes are made

3.   Keep fairy homes and pathways free from interference

4.   Don't interfere with devas' special plants and
                                    landscape features

5.   Maintain only good thoughts in the garden

6.   Keep fairy areas toxin and metal free

7.   Work the soil using wooden, bronze or copper tools

8.   Re-locate plant devas if necessary

**Chapter nine:
Divine gardening**

Chapter nine:
Divine gardening

"Enhancing the anima loci is a kind of spiritual gardening. It cannot result from attempts to command or control a place, but comes from participating consciously in the qualities already present, from which breathes an ennobling presence. The most important condition that we can establish there is an atmosphere of calm, peace, and emotional stability, so enabling us to be receptive to the divine." Nigel Pennick.

Temple Gardens

An image of paradise looks down from the author's kitchen wall, an antique Chinese Willow pattern plate, the likes of which once graced kitchens across all of Ireland. It's a classic image of a miniaturised landscape where nature is embraced and honoured. (The word paradise itself comes from the ancient Persian *pairidaeza*, meaning an enclosed or walled garden.)

Even so highly stylised, it conjures up the serenity of a Chinese Heaven on Earth, where curving waters flow and ripple, Willows bend and Bluebirds kiss in the sky above, all achieving balance and harmony of form together. One's eyes are drawn in to participate in a sacred landscape, into the Taoist world of reverance for nature, that was later adopted by Japanese Shintoists and Buddhists everywhere.

Here, people take their place in nature not as supreme dominators but as merely one part of a divine whole. This reverent attitude to nature has become most highly developed in the temple gardens of Kyoto, Japan.

In 1926 writer Laurens van der Post was one of the first Westerners to write about the Kyoto temple gardens. They were a revelation to him. He thought the most beautiful and significant of them to be the Temple of the Celestial Dragon, dating to the 13th century. It is also exceptional from having its conception influenced by a dream. Like other Japanese gardens, it was a far cry from gardens of the Western world, having no "ostentation or rhetoric and exhibitionism of flowers, or ornamental shrubbery… as remote as it could be from our obsession for imposing our own laws on, subduing and mastering nature for our own ends. It was the product of a profound and trusted partnership with the natural…. born of a love of nature in which each and everything had a shape, a validity and a right to maintain an inalienable dignity of its own. The gardener was the explorer of an inter-relationship, a secret sympathy, hidden in the profusion and diversity of nature, and so pledged to reproduce its underlying pattern on however small a scale so that the original design was there for the spirit to contemplate and follow." [1]

The spiritual qualities of such divine gardens invite the visitor to join, as van der Post put it, in the "process of discovery of the world within and a poetic grasp at its elusive meaning". No wonder those Willow pattern plates were so popular! They exude calm and sanctuary, harmony and geomantic balance. Just the thing for one's own Heavenly backyard. But how to translate them across? Well, you could incorporate some of the principles of Chinese geomancy, or feng shui.

Good feng shui in the garden

Feng shui offers an energetic approach to landscape design. The feng shui landscaper aims for an accumulation of vibrant ch'i energy in the garden, by sensitive and aesthetic design and placement of balanced elements, such as yin and yang features and the qualities of the five elements. (We will only consider the more ancient Form School approach to feng shui, which intuitively addresses the natural energetic qualities of landscape.)

In terms of yin/yang balance, both yin and yang ch'i is good to cultivate. Yin energy has a soothing, calming quality; while yang is more stimulating. Everything has both yin and yang energy in it, sometimes in balance, or else with a preponderance of one or the other. Plants and still waters bring more yin energy to a place, for example. Gushing streams or artificial waterfalls, rugged boulders and Towers of Power, will bring in more yang energy. An excess of yin or yang can create problems. So always check for the maximum size and number of Power Towers needed at a place, otherwise, if you have too many, you might become hyper-active from excessive yang! What is the ideal yin/yang ratio for a garden? For a stimulating environment with lush plant growth, the Chinese feng shui masters recommend to aim for three parts yang to two parts yin ch'i in a landscape.

Plants in general have a negative energetic charge and exude yin chi'. However there are always exceptions and yin and yang are relative qualities. Energetic investigations of the Oak finds one of the highest levels of electrical currents running through the trunk, while the wood itself is paramagnetic. Not surprisingly, dowsing finds a stimulating yang energy field around a healthy Oak tree, making it a good place to charge up one's energies. This is confirmation of ancient wisdom, that to spend time beneath an Oak tree can be highly energising.

In feng shui garden design, healthy and verdant trees in the right place will radiate excellent ch'i and also act as guardians of the home. (We already know that they can protect against geopathic energies, filter car fumes and electro-magnetic pollution to some extent too, so this is not surprising.) Evergreen trees are recommended for year round vibrancy and the bringing of good fortune. Thorny plants are best avoided.

However, too much vegetation crowded around a house, or big trees too close to the front door, can give an overbearing yin effect and block yang energies from entering. There is the practical aspect to this also, as tree roots can interfere with house foundations and drainage, or trees might block light from windows.

One maintains the good feng shui from your plants by pruning off any dead parts and keeping them healthy and happy. If plants are found to not be thriving in certain locations, it may be better to replace them with other species more suited to the site. Big old dead trees would be an exception to this if they have hollows that animals nest in. Rather than remove them it could be better to allow vines to cover their trunks or stumps for wildlife habitat.

Having accumulated an abundance of ch'i in the feng shui garden, the aim is to keep it moving freely around and not stagnating in tight corners or piles of clutter. So remove any barriers to ch'i flow and aim for a clutter-free garden. Make pathways wide enough for you to move easily along when plants on the edges are mature.

Don't let ch'i move too quickly through the garden, however. By designing paths, garden beds and waterways with curving forms, this helps to slow down ch'i flow to a healthy pace. Curving paths slow you down too and create more diverse views of scenery as you walk along them. They also increase the potential benefits of edge effect to plants. Make paths circulate freely around the garden and with no dead-ends.

Below: The Chinese Gardens, Sydney, Australia.

Good, strategically placed windbreaks are excellent too, as ch'i is blown away by too much wind. The term feng shui literally means 'wind and water'. Water and wind can build up ch'i, but too much of either can remove it. Windbreaks are often the first thing to be planted in a garden, to improve the microclimate. They can also be used, with proper placement, to symbolically represent mountain ranges. Typically, the north end of a site (in the northern hemisphere) would have the tree windbreak/'mountain range'. At the ends of this 'range' would ideally be 'lower slopes' (shorter trees or shrubs), altogether taking the auspicious form of an armchair shape. This form is also known as the 'mother embracing child' and if the house is placed in front, residents will be protected and nurtured. This is not only symbolically sound. The creation of sheltered microclimates is also good permaculture.

Besides mountains, the Chinese garden designers imitated nature by installing two other key landscape elements - woods and water. Obviously, we can't all have the real thing in our backyard, but they can of course be symbolically represented. The feng shui masters also aimed for a landscape balance of all five Chinese elements - of Wood, Water, Metal, Fire and Earth - for which some correspondences are listed overleaf. However, as the presence of metal is a no-no for the devas, the author has substituted it with the (European) element of Air. One might use this list to select feng shui features that could be appropriate or desirable. Or, if in doubt, try dowsing the list, first asking for which element/s need to be focussed on and then dowsing for the details.

Below: Ramping up the Fire element in a hot house in cool, moist Ireland.

Feng shui Landscaping List

Fire element
Tower of Power, pyramid, chimenea, clay oven, candles
Shapes - triangular
Colours - red and purple

Water element
Well, pond, bog garden, waterfall, bird bath, fountain, stream or spring
Shapes - wavy and horizontal
Colours - dark blue and black

Wood element
Upright plants, wooden structures / sculptures / furniture, totem pole
Shapes - rectangular
Colours - light and dark green

Earth element
Rocks, gravel, sand, terracotta and ceramics, stone paving and sculptures
Shapes - square
Colours - earthy, yellow and brown

Air element
Wind chimes, windmill, kinetic and sound sculptures, decorative mobiles, prayer flags and buntings, incense
Shapes - wisping
Colour - light blue and white

Mountain element
Standing stone, stone arrangement, hedge, tree grove, building, wall, trellis/screen, raised garden beds

Blessing seeds and plants

Prayer has long been advocated as a way to connect to the divine, to achieve problem solving or healing. So how much value does it have for people and their gardens? It has been affirmed by modern studies that prayer and blessings for human benefit are definitely effective. And this can also apply to gardeners. Since farming began, agricultural communities have created prayers and ceremony for all stages of crop production, to encourage soil, seeds and plants to thrive and be fruitful.

Nowadays uncommon in the Western world, the blessing of seeds and crops has been practised on the *Rogation Days* since medieval times. Rogation means praying or asking. Services are held to pray for plants and agricultural workers. In rural areas, people might also bless the fields, seeds and animals. In urban areas there is a blessing of gardens. Now no longer obligatory on the universal Roman Catholic Calendar, a local bishop might choose to follow the observance in some places.

The Major Rogation, or Rogation Sunday is held on April 25th, coinciding with St. Mark's Day; and the three days preceding Ascension Day (which used to be a Thursday) are the Minor Rogations, held between April 30th and June 3rd. Both Roman Catholic and Protestant churches once set them aside as days of abstinence and prayer, especially at the time of harvest. In many American churches Rogation Sunday is celebrated on the fifth Sunday after Easter and is otherwise called (since 1929) 'Rural Life Sunday' or 'Soil Stewardship Sunday'.

Rogation Days once also had a secular meaning in Britain, where they were called *Gang* or *Gange* Days, from the Saxon word gangen, meaning 'to go'. This involved a ritual walking of the parish boundaries during the three days before Holy Thursday (Ascension Day), with a procession of priests and prelates of the church, and a select number of men from the parish. The solemn processions were actually Christian adaptations of Roman pagan traditions. Later on, the Rogation Days were set aside for special local celebrations, such as in 19th-century Dorset, where a local festival, called the *Bezant*, was held annually on Rogation Monday. [2]

The working of the soil was also blessed in ancient cultures. In some areas, cider was poured as a libation onto newly ploughed soil, while love-making in thrice-ploughed field furrows has anciently been a popular pastime for benefiting the future crop. The goddess Demeter, it seems, was the first to initiate this symbolic soil fertilising method.

In Herefordshire, UK, each year on May Day morning seedbeds were once decorated with crosses of Rowan and Birch branchlets, placed as an invocation of protection and productivity. [3] In Irish tradition, people would sprinkle St Brigit's Holy Well water as a blessing, for protection around their homes and on the seeds for next season's crops. This is probably still practised by some rural people. The water is ideally collected on St. Brigit's feast day of February 1st, the start of spring and date of the annual pilgrimage to the Wells.

There are many such St. Brigit's Holy Wells in Ireland, but the custom of pilgrimage to them has almost died out. The author went to one on St Brigit's Day 2016, near Ballinamore in County Leitrim. It was a rather sombre affair, with people walking in silence or uttering prayers quietly. In the sacred tree grove around this well they did their rounds, drank the water (as on the left) and filled bottles to bring more home with them. [4]

Firey blessings were given to the crops when Scottish farmers bearing flaming torches of Fir wood once circumnavigated their fields on a sunwise course. This also happened in Ireland at mid-summer, when people gathered at Knockaine, hill of sun goddess Aine in County Limerick, to run through the fields of grain at midnight, waving their flaming brands to stimulate the ripening of the corn and invoke the goddess's blessing. [5] Summer sun in northern climates can be a fickle mistress and needs all the encouragement she can get!

When planting valuable trees in Britain, votive offerings were once given. These were often of a practical nature, such as a lamb's newly removed tail at docking time that was placed under Poplar trees in Yorkshire. At planting time, gold coins were once placed beneath Walnut trees in Suffolk; while pieces of coal were put under Perry Pear trees in Gloucestershire. [3]

Harvest and thanksgiving

Giving thanks for Earth's bounty is an ancient concept that puts people in their proper place, co-dependent with Mother Nature. In the old nature-friendly ways, when you harvested something from a plant you would be expected to make an offering of thanks in return for the plant's gift. This might be a bit of food, a glass of enhanced water, a heartfelt prayer or a promise of some future action such as the plant's protective care and nourishment. The author likes to do a little weeding around a plant that's being harvested and generally tending to it's needs.

In Russia, country herbalists heading off to harvest herbs would traditionally ask permission to begin with. They would say: *"Mother Earth grant me your blessing to gather some of your herbs."* [6] And in Ireland in early August, at Lughnasa - the festival at the start of harvest and end of summer, there were traditions of the hilltop burial of flowers. [7] This symbolic giving of tithes back to the Earth was once considered obligatory for the ensuing harvest.

The Christian Rogation days were also a time for people to express gratitude for soil, water and plant growth. Asking and thanking are two sides of the same coin. It is the act of giving thanks that provides another opportunity for sincere connection with plant spirits. Gratitude is a healing quality to develop in ourselves and it also helps to gain the devas' respect. It truly is the thought that counts!

Ceremonies at harvest time

Long ago, herbalists knew to cut their herbs during certain phases of the Sun and Moon, when their potency was maximised. They would have enacted harvest rituals too. In a well known example, Druids of Europe's woodlands harvested the sacred Mistletoe plant from its Oak tree host only at the correct Moon time. This was done without the use of iron, using only a golden knife or sickle, as mentioned by Pliny and written about in Sir James Frazer's famous tome 'The Golden Bough'. The best days for this was Midsummer's Eve or Day, or on May Day. If Mistletoe was needed for ritual use, the Druids, dressed in white, let it drop into a cloth to prevent it from touching the ground. Before this was done, an offering of bread and wine was made. [8]

The ancient Romans were also very careful when harvesting their herbs, such as Sage, that they treasured as sacred for it's healing effects on the brain and throat. With due ceremony, wearing clean clothes and with clean feet, the Roman Sage gatherer would first make a sacrifice of food. They would also use a special knife that was not made from iron, as Sage reacts with iron salts and is tainted by it. [9]

By creating our own ceremonies to honour plants at harvest time, we play our part in the Great Deal. We honour that they sacrifice their lives to us, trusting that we will be the agents of their resurrection in the seasons that follow. This life-and-death cycle was personified each harvest time by the early Anglo-Saxons as the sacrificial death of John Barleycorn, who must have once been their corn god.

A small herb, a 'weed' that the author allowed to grow and fully express itself in the garden, reminded me of this. As I looked down kindly at it, it gave me the thought: "Don't forget to write about the Deal that we plants make with mankind." Yes, of course. Food growing is about give-and-take in equal measure and mankind needs to remember this! We should not poison the soil or the food will poison us. Ideally, we feed the soil organically so that it may feed us wholesomely. And we tend our divine gardens as well as we would tend ourselves.

Effects of sound and dance

It is widely known that plants respond positively to certain music. They especially enjoy Baroque and Indian sacred music. Studies of the effects of music and dance on enhancing plant growth rates by T.C.N. Singh at the Bihar Agricultural College in India found that Indian ragas and dancing around plants really did improve their health and growth levels.

In Europe there are surviving customs of tree singing and honouring, such as the British tradition of *wassailing*. People would gather around the best bearing Apple trees at the end of winter to toast the tree's health and fecundity for the following year. They would sing simple songs and dirge chants to praise the tree, or even threaten to uproot it if the next harvest wasn't good! They sometimes danced in a circle around the tree and gave it an offering of cider, toast or roasted apples. In Sussex they bowed to the trees. Lots of cider was consumed by people too and it was a time for great revelry. They sometimes made lots of noise, even firing guns over the tree to 'wake it up', or to 'chase off evil spirits' - perhaps to deter pests.

In Devonshire a little boy was hoisted up the tree, to act as a personification of 'The Robin', in other words the tree spirit. With the call - *'Tit, tit, I want something to eat'* - he would be handed up some bread, cheese and cider. [10] This certainly harks back to pagan times. Wassailing is being taken up again, especially by ardent cider drinkers, one imagines.

It seems odd to be stimulating Apple trees in the middle of their dormant period. Any excuse for some revelry, one supposes. However it is known that planetary forces are being registered by trees during hibernation, as seen in the resonant pulsations of their buds. And elsewhere also, trees are being focussed on at that time of year. Over in rural Russia, an ancient tradition for new year involves shaking snow from the branches of Apple trees to ensure a good harvest in the following year. [6]

Singing to your plants generally is known to produce significantly enhanced plant growth. Traditional Hopi Indian farmers have long practised this. Sessions of drumming in the Men of the Trees plant nursery in Perth, Australia, likewise gave good results, in experiments conducted there. Singing, being hands-free, is probably the more practical option. Knowing that chanting, playing music, or singing brings much joy and stimulus to plants and their devas, one might be guided by the words of house spirit Miller, who told von Holstein:

"We love it when humans play music. You can also sing us a song. It doesn't have to be a complicated aria, a simple children's song will do." [11]

Garden altars and spirit houses

Where to enact our garden rituals or deva connection? An altar or spirit house could be erected. These are found in profusion in Hindu and Buddhist communities of India and Asia, in backyards and shop fronts, on roadsides and building sites (where workers may refuse to work until one is installed, for fear of accidents generated by unhappy devas). Spirit houses on the ground are for honouring Earth spirits, while ones placed higher up, sometimes in trees, are for the Air spirits.

Right - Air spirit shrine, Malaysia.

Not that you need to have anything special to achieve deva connection. However if you do have a special stone or rock outcrop, an ancient tree or a cave or ferny nook, these may well serve as ideal locations to connect with the garden devas. If you don't have such features, you might create stone arrangements. These can become excellent anchors for nature beings, who often form attachments to rocks. Altars can also be made out of many other things. Just avoid metals! Metal interrupts the flow of subtle energies and disturbs the fairies.

It will be your regular activities at this altar that will make it special. It helps to have a place for you to sit there too, a special bench for meditation and prayer is a good idea. Dowse for where the altar is best located. The spirits of place often have firm views on where this should be. It's a good idea to ask the chief garden spirit first, or use dowsing.

Once you have set the intention for your altar or spirit house, the site will evolve over time and you will probably make adjustments and

improvements. An initial blessing ceremony is good and if you decide to move it to another part of the garden later on, have a little ceremony first to explain this to the devas. Regularity of use will help to build up the ch'i in the area around it.

Left: Earth spirit shrine beside a city street, Kerala, India.

"As the vibe of your garden rises," Madis Senner wrote of using garden altars, "several things will begin to happen. You will start to develop sentience of Mother Earth and she will begin revealing herself. Just as looking within ourselves brings answers, intuitions and revelations, so too will an altar area of a garden do the same with Mother Earth, only the fruit will be a greater awareness of her and your garden." [12]

A physical prop to connect with the Otherworlds is not strictly necessary, of course. What is inside of you, in your thoughts and feelings, is what counts the most. Some people may be unused to the concept and feel uneasy about an altar or get the wrong idea. Even nature spirits can be wary of altars, as conveyed to von Holstein by the dryad Miller, who told her: "Please, don't raise any altars to us. That's not the right way. Altars are for gods, not nature beings." [11]

You can put out deva offerings at any place and any time. When asked what type of offerings would be appreciated by nature-beings, Miller spoke about the ancient custom of giving libations, calling it:

"a beautiful custom...giving a little of what one was drinking to the nature-beings." A little liquid is offered to nature, by pouring a few drops on the ground. As simple as that.

"What matters most here," Miller said, "is the gesture of sacrifice. The point is to give away something that you as a human are fond of... Give something that you like most and put it somewhere until it goes mouldy. A somewhat larger meal can be put out on definite days or as a thankyou because something worked out very well."

Gardening magic in the Pacific Islands

Maori people of New Zealand are excellent farmers and gardeners. To engage the assistance of the agricultural deities, they would traditionally erect focal points in their fields. Made of stone and wood, these became anchor points for the *atua* and *mauri* (- resting place of the life principle) to reside in the garden. Here, at crop planting in springtime and also at harvest time, the *tohunga* (medicine man) would recite ritual chants to encourage increase of the crop. And if rain was needed, a wooden bullroarer would be ritually employed to bring rain to the crops.

In the delightful legend of the first sweet potato, Rongo, the god of cultivated crops as well as of peace, mated with goddess Te Pani, the Earth Mother, and from that union Kumara, the peace child, the Sweet Potato, was born. Keeping the peace child growing peacefully, the Waitaha tradition allowed sadness or anger no place in the garden. Growing the sacred crop was a joyful occupation.

Stone carvings of Rongo were used as a representative of the god. When placed in gardens they ensured greater fertility of the crops and success of the harvest. Statues of Rongo's wife Te Pani were also placed there, so that she could watch over crops, with her characteristic wide eyes to search for poor seed, her big head for wisdom and rotund body to encourage bulky tuber growth. Both deities had offerings made to them.

The garden godstone is a tradition seen Pacific-wide, including several statues recorded from remote Pitcairn Island. Godstones were typically around 12–18 inches (30–45 centimetres) high and depicted a very rotund figure with short arms and only three fingers. In wintertime these

godstones (one is seen on the left) were kept at the *tuaha* (sacred keeping place), or concealed elsewhere. Here they stayed until taken back to the garden at planting time, where they would be set up again at the head of the field.

When it was time to plant the kumara and to ensure a good crop, the tohunga would call upon Rongo to take up residence in the statue. During planting, an appeal would be made to Te Pani – '*Oh Pani – pour out thy basket on this field*'. A favourite planting time was Orongonui, the 28th day of the moon cycle and named after Rongo. When a field was to be planted and prior to the special karakia (ritual) necessary for that, four special wooden godsticks provided by a tohunga would also be stuck in the ground, one at each corner of the field. Godsticks were used in many rites. In other parts of the Pacific, such as Tahiti and Rarotonga, godsticks represented a hybrid god Rongo-ma-Tane, combining the god of cultivated plants with Tane, the god of wild forests.

The Trobriand Islanders had similar traditions of garden magic. Their shamen would strike the garden with a sacred wooden wand, symbolic of the magician's office, to impart fertilising energy. Miniature houses of spirits and stakes of the spirits would be placed in Trobriand gardens. Other small sticks put in gardens acted as signs, warning that a taboo of not gardening was in force, such as when a sacred ceremony was scheduled. [13]

Garden sanctuary
by Kate Wimble, NSW, Australia

"I went to my sanctuary space here by a great Pine tree to spend the night with Nature. After a while this being's face emerged in the tree, looking like an ancient gnome/Earth elemental, very sombre and just observing me.

"Since then I reconnected and he says he is called Rufus. He also says I can engage him to heal my Olive orchard. And engage him in my Earth energy work, especially in drawing energy from the Earth to radiate out, to give vital energy to all out there. Wow, what a connection!!"

Creating sacred sites

Traditionally the most revered elements of landscape are the unusual or striking yang features, such as mountain tops, special boulders or mighty trees; and the hidden and mysterious yin features - the caves, lakes and secret places. Ancient sacred sites can also look fairly ordinary, to an outsider's eyes at least. But energetically they can be very special. At some sacred sites, studies have found that magnetic fields in the brain are greatly stirred up and this can facilitate visionary experiences. Many people also experience healing at sacred sites too.

While we need to fully value and treasure ancient sites and protect them vigorously, it's more sustainable for the planet to create our own sacred centres. Then we don't need to go on a trip to Egypt to experience the divine and mysterious. We can pilgrimage into our own backyards!

A sanctuary for communion with Mother Nature, Earth and Cosmos that is regularly interacted with can elevate the ch'i level of a place. The love you bring to such a place can be amplified manifold. Being there can take you into sublime, altered states of being.

Sacred trees and groves can be planted again. One might also create minilithic monuments, placing special stones at certain locations selected by dowsing. Stones placed in the landscape provide a solid means of anchoring our intentions, as well as being 'deva magnets'. Crystalline structures in certain rocks, such as quartz and feldspar, have a powerful ability to retain and convey energies and memory, and you might want to programme your intentions into them. The selection process for feature stones could also look at the yin (eg quartz) or yang (eg basalt) qualities that you want to invoke also.

Always check first if particular rock energies are going to be suitable for your sacred space. Be aware that rocks found in the 'wild', as well as harbouring wildlife beneath them, will probably object to being moved. Before taking rocks, always ask for their permission. It's usually best to leave surface rocks where they belong. A quarry might well be the best source.

Stones large and small are great for creating labyrinths and stone circles, and their best locations can be found by dowsing. Such stone arrangements can be energised with rituals, such as a walking meditation in a stone circle. This can increase or harmonise energy in the garden for all to benefit from. The good energy generated can radiate out into the wider region as well.

Stone circles make strong deva magnets. The author finds guardian spirits stationed in the centre of stone circles both old and new. For example, two small stone circles, one of milky white quartz river washed stones and the other of pink granite, were made on the author's farm in Australia. (The stones used were around 20-30 centimetres/8-12 inches in diameter.) Soon afterwards Earth elemental beings moved into them. Surrounding plants began to grow much more vigorously around the circles and growth became lush all around. The devas remained happily stationed there, one residing in the centre of each of the stone circles, mostly under the ground.

Interactive use of stone arrangements can result in the attraction of other sorts of energies to them as well. British dowsers have reported cases of underground water lines that are are found to appear, moving in slowly from elsewhere, over the course of around three months. This could mean that water flows may end up coursing beneath your sleeping place, a potentially hazardous outcome. So it may not be best to locate a powerful circle or labyrinth too close to the house, to avoid any intense energy exposure in the home. Dowse the idea first! [14]

Power Towers, symbolic of the Fire element, can provide control points from where we broadcast our intentions. They can also give the devas a buzz! Often an Air elemental deva can be detected attached to the top of a Power Tower, the author finds. When dowsing Irish Round Towers, very much larger versions that originally inspired the Power Towers, I have sometimes found enormous devas stationed at them.

To keep the high energy maintained, one needs to boost Power Tower

energies with regular rituals, that are ideally done around the time of the full moon. Otherwise the energy field will diminish somewhat. A blessing ceremony (as on the left) can be a great event, especially if a group of friends plus music, song or dance are involved! This is a good time to re-programme new intentions into the field, as the seasons change.

For a more yin energy sacred site you might create a beautiful pond with yin rocks, such as white quartz or limestone,

and plant it out with flowering aquatic plants. It would be a great place for peaceful contemplation. A pond plus cascade, or a *flow-form* with water that is pumped through it, can be pretty enlivening too and a bit more yang. Whatever you want to do, always 'check-in' first with the spirits of place.

Fairyfield dreaming

At the author's new home, an old stone cottage on two acres (about one hectare) in Ireland, I was kept busy for the first year building garden beds, planting a woodland and caring for existing trees that had been neglected. One of the fields is a fairy hot-spot and I got to know the queen of the 'tribe'. Juliana, as I call her, is a gracious, tiny being some 60 centimetres (two feet) tall. Her home is in the Underworld, down a Fairy Hole (geo-vortex). A serpentine Fairy Line leads into this vortex, the same one that I wrote about in the book 'Sensitive Permaculture'. A ring of Oak trees have now been planted around the Fairy Hole and a small stone circle made around it too, as seen below. Small stones, some with fossils, that were found around the house and fields, possibly glacial erratics from afar that dropped in during the Ice Age, were used for the circle. They are handy to sit on.

Back in late winter my morning meditations of blessing the land had detected a 'gate crasher'. I started to see, in my 'mind's eye', the head of a large female nature being that would pop up from under the ground to join us, her eyes closed in some sort of meditative or semi-dormant state. I didn't pay much attention to this being at first. Meanwhile there was a huge amount of damp in the old cottage and I wasn't sure why. Eventually I was able to learn from this deva that she was a water spirit, normally of underground waters, but as the whole place was awash I wasn't surprised to meet her in the house. I eventually worked out that the field above the house had defunct drains and so we were receiving the water that ran off it from fields higher up. A bit of earthworks was needed to sort it out, when the land was drier. I told the water spirit the plan to improve the drains, make a beautiful pond and later clear out the old seepage well that once must have serviced several families as a water supply. I asked her to do a deal with me. In exchange for my improvement of the water ways in the landscape, would she please withdraw the waters that were flowing into the house area? She seemed happy enough to help.

The improved drainage was eventually done and it brought an end to the damp problem in the house. The water devi never came into the house again. Instead, she moved into the new pond (seen on the right) and when I 'visited' in my morning meditations she was always there, lying blissful and motionless in the water. She remained silent and static, but over the months became more responsive to my blessings and started to open her eyes a bit.

At mid-summer I told my deva friends the plan to erect a small Tower of Power in their field. Of course they had no idea what a Power Tower was. I was keen to encourage the newly planted woodland to grow fast and assumed all would go well. Assumption is always a dangerous thing! The Power Tower, after activation, had a powerful energy field that filled up around one acre in area (4,000 square metres). The students who helped to make it were buzzing and so was I.

But the next day, when I tuned into the Fairyfield devas, I realised that it was all a bit too much, too soon for some. Juliana was overcome by the energy, rather bewildered and cranky. She was also some three of four times her original size, talk about pumped up! I had a bit of explaining to do! It took several days of *fairy whispering* before she settled down, but she seemed to accept the new energy then. As for the water spirit, when I tuned into her after the Tower went up, she was standing up tall in her pond and dancing! A few days later I saw that she was singing! She made happy toning-like sounds, with single clear notes ringing out. She was somewhat bigger too. From then on she was always dancing and singing when I visited her through the days of summer and into the mild autumn (at the time of writing).

Going back to before the Tower went up, one day when meditating in the stone circle I had clairvoyantly looked down into the geo-vortex and made a nice discovery. There I saw a blue and white dragon, a serpentine being acting as a guardian of place. Friendly enough, it later showed itself to me coiled around the central energy shaft of the vortex, spinning around, churning with the energy. The image of this churning motion reminded me of the ancient Hindu creation story, where the great snake Shesha churned up an ocean of milk in the Heavens to make Soma, elixir of immortality. Sesha tore up Mount Mandara to use it as a churning rod and he got another giant snake being, Vasuki, to coil around this 'rod' and act as the churning rope. Primordial stuff!

After the Power Tower was erected, I saw that the blue and white dragon was very happy with the new energy. And checking the Tower, I found another smaller dragon was now stationed there, wrapped around this new 'churning rod', enjoying the buzz of the vortical Tower energies and probably feeding off them too. So, no worries there. It seems that you can please some of the devas some of the time, but you can't always please all of the devas all of the time!

Two months passed and the growth of woodland trees in the field was quite remarkable! Many had doubled in size in the five months since planting, as pointed out by visitors. The devas are big and happy and have settled down. There's a bright, magical feeling to the field. And now that there is also a resident Leshy, with the spiritual know-how to care for a woodland, I look forwards to future forest adventures with my deva friends.

What if you don't have a garden?

When we practise eco-sensitivity and garden with the welfare of the plant spirits in mind, Mother Nature can help to soothe our stresses and heal our ails. Divine gardening can be a pure pleasure of enjoyment and creativity too. We can find in it the bliss that is so elusive in the world of concrete and steel. So gardening is also a great metaphor for nurturing the inner self.

You don't even need to have a garden of your own. Mother Nature and your own true nature can provide you with the space. As house spirit Miller suggested to von Holstein, when asked about keeping street trees healthy: "You can choose a tree in the town and say 'Good Morning' to it every day. That'll help the tree a lot. You should do it at least once a week. When it's very hot you can also bring it a bucket of water. In this way you start a tree sponsorship programme." [11]

Otherwise you might like to adopt the garden of a derelict house, or farm the patch of dirt on the roadside in front of your house and transform it into a public food garden. You could become a guerilla gardener and seed trees in trashy urban wasteland areas. Or attend permaculture blitzes, working on other people's gardens, or take on a garden allotment - these introduce a social aspect as well. You don't have to own property to be a true gardener. The devas are always delighted when we do something that brings beauty, bio-diversity and fertility to any place (especially a sad or traumatised place).

And you can garden on an inner level too. In your imagination you can create a sacred green sanctuary. It could be a therapeutic garden, a grove on a hilltop or around a sacred well, or a formoyle (- a meadow of healing herbs), or all of the above. Here you can retreat and re-create yourself whenever you wish. When life is stressful - sit back, slow down, close your eyes and deepen your breathing. Imagine you are walking down a meandering garden path, admiring the flowers, shrubs and vegetables growing there. Taking in the soothing greens and stimulating flower colours. You walk in a reverent state of pilgrimage and your senses are engaged by the sights and smells.

Overleaf: The grove at St Patrick's Well, Killargue, Co. Roscommon, Ireland.

Eventually you arrive at your Sacred Grove, at a gateway portal. Here you might place a little gift of gratitude on a special stone beside the path. Then enter your nemeton and take in the beauty of the circular space, the lush green trees growing in a ring around you, the sky bright above. Here you might lay on the soft grass and watch towering trees waving in the breeze and listen to your favourite birdsong. Or sit beside an earthing stone and hold it with both hands to allow the release of any pent up energies. Or sip waters from your well. Anything is possible!

So you see that divine gardening is really a state of mind. We cultivate the power of loving-kindness, patience and gratitude within ourselves. We practise this by making loving connections with the plants around us. This can deeply nourish the growth of our own souls and we go on to harvest the grace and beauty of nature.   Happy gardening!

Divine Gardening Summary

1. Design the garden to be energetically harmonious, with a good balance of yin and yang ch'i and the Elements.

2. Encourage the healthy, natural fertility of plants, soil, fungi, microbes and animals.

3. Make the garden a haven for yourself too - let it be a beautiful, creative, inspiring and healing place where you can get well grounded.

4. Create and protect Deva Stations and green corridors for fairy and wildlife habitat and movement.

5. Connect to the devas at special places, stone arrangements, garden altars or spirit houses.

6. Practise rituals of blessing at seed sowing and planting times.

7. Talk sweetly to plants and as they grow, joyfully sing, dance and make music in your garden.

8. At harvest time express heart-felt thanks, or create ceremonies to honour plants.

References

Chapter one:

1. Carey, Tony, 'Confessions of a Climate Alarmist', in Crann - Ireland's Tree Magazine, spring/summer 2015, issue 101.
2. Mildrexler, David J et al, 'A global comparison between station air temperature and MODIS land surface temperatures reveals the cooling role of forests', Journal of Geophysical Research, vol. 116, August 2011. Via Crann, Ireland's Tree Magazine issue no. 103 summer 2016.
3. Hageneder, Fred, 'The Spirit of Trees - Science, Symbiosis and Inspiration', Floris Books, UK, 2000.
4. Cook, Roger, 'The Tree of Life, symbol at the centre', Thames and Hudson, London, UK 1974.
5. Webster, Graham, 'The British Celts and their Gods under Rome', Batsford, London, 1986.
6. From - http://www.pbase.com/neuenhofer/naga_cult_in_tamil_nadu
7. Stamets, Paul, 'Mycelium Running - how mushrooms can help save the world', Ten Speed Press, 2005, Berkeley, USA.
8. http://www.abc.net.au/science/articles/2015/05/20/4236600.htm
9. Wohlleben, Peter, 'The Hidden Life of Trees: What They Feel, How They Communicate — Discoveries From a Secret World', Greystone Books, UK, 2016. Extracted from -
http://www.nytimes.com/column/the-saturday-profile Jan. 29th, 2016.
10. From - http://www.care2.com/causes/go-on-hug-a-tree-it-might-be-good-for-you.html#ixzz2WQUQwtrn
Also - http://www.trueactivist.com/science-proves-hugging-trees-is-good-for-health/ June 23rd, 2014.
11. Haxeltine, Michael, 'Trees, Town Planning, Health and Subtle Energies', self published 2010, UK.
12. Crann, Ireland's Tree magazine, autumn/winter issue 2015, no 102.
Also see www.naturehealthandwellbeing.ie

Chapter two:

1. Hodson, Geoffrey, 'Fairies at Work and at Play', Theosophical Publishing, USA, 1982.
2. Van Gelder, Dora, 'The Real World of Fairies - a first person account', Quest Books, USA, 1977.
3. Maclagan, David, 'Creation Myths - man's introduction to the world', Thames and Hudson, London, 1977.
4. http://www.theoi.com/Olympios/DemeterTreasures.html
5. MacNeill, Mairie, 'The Festival of Lughnasa', University College, Dublin, 1962.
6. Smith, William (ed), 'Dictionary of Greek and Roman Biography and Mythology', Little, Brown and Co, Boston, USA, 1844.
7. Aksit, Ilhan, 'The Aegean Mythology- the story of the two sides', Republic of Turkey Ministry of Culture and Tourism General Directorate of Libraries and Publications, Istanbul 2010.
8. Moore, Alanna, 'Divining Earth Spirit', Python Press, Australia, 2004.
9. Wallis Budge, E. A., 'Egyptian Ideas of the Future Life', chapter 2, originally published 1900. Via - http://en.wikipedia.org/wiki/Osiris
10. Indigenous Songlines- http://www.abc.net.au/news/2016-07-04/naidoc-week-indigenous-songlines/75576542
11. Aburrow, Yvonne, 'The Enchanted Forest - the magical lore of trees', Capall Ban, UK, 1993.
12. Ketels, Maxwell, 'Piper at the Gates of Dawn - The Historic and Symbolic Pan', based on lecture given to the Carl Jung Society of Melbourne.
13. Moore, Alanna, 'Resurgence of the Green Man', Geomantica magazine no. 23, March 2004. In Geomantica Archives, www.geomantica.com
14. Mac Coitir, Niall, 'Irish Trees - myths, legends, & folklore', The Collins Press, 2003, Ireland.
15. Waterson, Roxanne, 'The Living House', Oxford University Press, UK, 1990.
16. Weirauch, Wolfgang (ed.), 'Nature Spirits and what they say - interviews with Verena Stael von Holstein', Floris Books, 2004, UK.
17. Simon, Ben, 'Tales, Traditions and Folklore of Ireland's Trees', The Forest of Belfast, 2012, Northern Ireland.
18. Buckler, Nicole, 'Celtic Trees of Worship', 'The Genuine Irish Old Moore's Almanac 2016', Ireland.
19. Gilchrist, Cherry, 'Russian Magic - living traditions of an enchanted landscape', Quest Books, USA, 2009.
20. Moore, Alanna, 'Helping the Devas'. A short Geomantica film of interviews with Swedish dowsers about working with the forest devas. See at - https://www.youtube.com/watch?v=jApDqWhv0oY

Chapter three:

1. Narby, Jeremy, 'The Cosmic Serpent - DNA and the Origins of Knowledge', 1998, W & N, USA.
2. Cowan, Eliot, 'Plant Spirit Medicine - a journey into the healing wisdom of plants', Sounds True, USA, 2nd edition 2004.
3. Messegue, Maurice, 'Of People and Plants', Macmillan, 1972 UK.
4. Gregory, Lady, 'Visions and Beliefs in the West of Ireland', Colin Smythe, Gerrards Cross UK, 1920.
5. O'Hanlon, Rev. John, 'Irish Folklore', 1870, EP Publishing, UK.
6. Mac Garraidhe, Murt, 'Strangers at Home', Kilmore Quay Publications, Ireland 2009.
7. Bord, Janet, 'The Travellers Guide to Fairy Sites - the landscape and folklore fairyland in England, Wales and Scotland', Gothic Image, UK, 2004.
8. O'Connor, Tom, 'Hand of History, Burden of Pseudo History', Trafford, Ireland, 2005.
9. O'Donovan, John, 'Ordinance Survey Letters Roscommon - letters relating to the antiquities of the County Roscommon containing information collected during the progress of the Ordnance Survey in 1837', Fourmasters Press, Dublin, 2010.
10. Moore, Alanna, 'Herb Lore, Fairies and Seers in Old Ireland', Geomantica no 59. In Geomantica Archives at www.geomantica.com .
11. 'Social and Therapeutic Horticulture: evidence and messages from research', Centre for Child & Family Research, UK (Loughborough University).
12. Thrive (2008) 'Harnessing the mood-boosting power of gardening. How can gardening improve my emotional well-being?' Geoffrey Udall Centre, Beech Hill, Reading, UK.
13. Haller R and Kramer C, (eds) 'Horticultural Therapy Methods - making connections in health care, human service and community programs,' The Haworth Press, UK, 2006.
14. 'Therapeutic Garden Characteristics', American Horticultural Therapy Association quarterly publication, volume 41, no. 2.

Chapter four:

1. Moore, Alanna, 'Divining Earth Spirit', Python Press, 2004, Australia.

2. Fox, Selena, 'Herb Craft', Circle Network News, Sept. 1980, USA.

3. Moore, Alanna, 'Flower Power!' Geomantica magazine no. 20, June 2003.

4. Schorr-kon, Thomas, 'Bountiful Birch the Bright Tree', Permaculture magazine, issue 20, UK.

5. Tompkins, Peter and Bird, Christopher, 'The Secret Life of Plants', Allen Lane, London, 1973.

6. Gardenia, Tigrilla, 'Damanhur and the Music of the Plants', Caduceus magazine, issue 90, Nov-Dec 2015, UK, online.

7. Bond PhD, Hilary, 'The Plant Spirits of Place: Tree Spirit Wars in an Outback Community', manuscript, Australia, 2016.

8. Kindred, Glennie, 'The Sacred Tree', self published, UK, 1995.

9. Geo, Dr. 'Angels of Canberra', online at http://chisync.com/Geo/Angels%20Of%20Canberra/Angels%20in%20 Canberra%20Australia.htm

Chapter five:

1. Hageneder, Fred, 'The Spirit of Trees - science, symbiosis and inspiration', Floris Books, Scotland, 2000.

2. Extracted from: http://www.abc.net.au/science/articles/2013/02/22/3696146.htm?site= science&topic=latest

3. http://www.telegraph.co.uk/news/obituaries/9146710/Maria-Thun.html

4. Callahan, Prof. Philip S., 'Paramagnetism - rediscovering nature's secret force of growth', Acres USA, 1995.

5. http://www.spiritofmaat.com/archive/aug3/korotkov.htm

6. Ross, T. Edward, 'A Dowser's Model', American Society of Dowsers' Journal, vol 23, no. 2, May 1983.

7. Steiner, Rudolph, 'Nature Spirits - selected lectures', Rudolph Steiner Press, UK, 1995.

8. Van Gelder, Dora, 'The Real World of Fairies - a first person account', Quest Books, USA, 1977.

9. Haxeltine, Michael, 'Trees, Town Planning, Health and Subtle Energies', self published 2010, UK.

10. Hodson, Geoffrey, 'The Kingdom of the Gods', Theosophical Publishing House 1952, USA.

11. Pogacnik, Marko, 'Nature Spirits and Elemental Beings',

Findhorn Press, Scotland, 1995.
12. Weirauch, Wolfgang (ed.), 'Nature Spirits and what they say - interviews with Verena Stael von Holstein', Floris Books, 2004, UK.
13. Goldsmith, Edward, The Vision of St. Barbe-Baker
Article at www.edwardgoldsmith.org/927/richard-st-barbe-baker/
14 Glaser, PhD, Zorach R., 'Naval Medical Research Institute - Bibliography of reported biological phenomena ('effects) and clinical manifestations attributed to microwave and radio-frequency radiation', Project MF12.524.015-0004B, Report no.2, April 1972, National Naval Medical Centre, Bethesda, Maryland, 2014, USA.
15. Kolodynski and Kolodynska, 'Motor and psychological functions of school children lliving in the area of the Skrunda Radio Location Station in Latvia', The Science of the Total Environment 180:88-93, 1996.)
16. Philips, Alasdair and Jean, 'Mobile Phones and Masts, the Health Risks', Powerwatch Publications, June 2004, UK.
17. Jamieson, Dr Isaac, 'Smart Meters – Smarter Practices' (Jamieson, 2011, pp. 137-144) via Stop Smart Meters Australia.
18. 'Is Wi-Fi Killing Trees?' 18th November 2015 at http://wakeup-world.com/2015/11/18/is-wi-fi-killing-trees/
19. Cammaerts MC and Johansson O, 'Phyton, International Journal of Experimental Botany', 84: 132-137, 2015. Via EMR and Health - Vol 12 No 1 March 2016. See www.emraustralia.com.au

Chapter six:

1. Aziz, Peter, 'Working with Tree Spirits in Shamanic Healing', Points Press, UK, 1994.
2. Haxeltine, Michael J, 'Trees, Town Planning, Health and Subtle Energies', manuscript, UK, 2010.
3. Hodson, Geoffrey, 'Kingdom of the Gods', Theosophical Publishing House, USA, 1952.
4. Hodson, Geoffrey, 'Fairies at Work and at Play', Theosophical Publishing, USA, 1982.
5. Ross, T. Edwards, 'A Dowser's Model', in the American Society of Dowsers Journal, vol 23, no 2, May 1983.

Chapter seven:

1. Moore, Alanna, 'The Wisdom of Water', Python Press, Australia, 2007. Moore, Alanna, 'Divining Earth Spirit', Python Press, Australia, 2004.
2. Moore, Alanna, 'Stone Age Farming', Python Press, 2001, Australia. (Also in American, Chinese and German editions.)
3. Ober, Clint, Sinatra MD, Stephen, and Zucker, Martin, 'Earthing - the most important health discovery ever?', Basic Health Publications, 2010, USA.

Chapter eight:

1. Gregory, Lady, 'Visions and Beliefs in the West of Ireland', Colin Smythe Gerrards Cross, UK, 1920.
2. van Gelder, Dora, 'The Real World of Fairies - a first person account', Quest Books, USA, 1977.
3. Machaelle Small-Wright, The Perelandra Garden Workbook', Perelandra Ltd. USA, 1987.
4. Whitman, John, 'The Psychic Power of Plants,' Star Books, 1975, UK.
5. http://www.teara.govt.nz/en/te-waonui-a-tane-forest-mythology/page-1
6. Leisa India, Dec. 2012 and India-Rio20. At: http://www.environment.brahmakumaris.org/component/content/catego ry/40-yogic-agriculture
7. Moore, Alanna, 'Touchstones for Today', Python Press, 2013, Australia.
8. Source: www.implementations.co.uk

Chapter nine:

Pennick, Nigel, 'Celtic Sacred Landscapes', Thames and Hudson, London, 1996.
1. van der Post, Laurens, 'Yet Being Someone Other', Hogarth Press, UK, 1982.
2. http://encyclopedia2.thefreedictionary.com/Rogation+Sunday
3. Aburrow, Yvonne, 'The Sacred Grove, Mysteries of the Forest', 1994, Capall Bann, UK.

4. Moore, Alanna, 'Irish Holy Well Pilgrimage 2016', Geomantica magazine no. 64 February 2016. Geomantica Archives, www.geomantica.com

5. Dames, Michael, 'Mythic Ireland', Thames &Hudson, UK, 1992

6. Gilchrist, Cheryl, 'Russian Magic - living folk traditions of an enchanted landscape' Quest Books, 2009, USA.

7. NacNeill, Mairie, 'The Festival of Lughnasa', University College, Dublin, Ireland, 1962.

8. Baker, Margaret, 'Discovering the Folklore of Plants', Shire Publications, UK, 2013.

9. McVicar, Jekka, 'Jekka's Complete Herb Book' Kyle Books, UK, 2007.

10. Cater, Colin and Cater, Karen, 'Wassailing - reawakening an ancient folk tradition', Hedingham Fair, 2013, UK.

11. Weirauch, Wolfgang (ed.), 'Nature Spirits and what they say - interviews with Verena Stael von Holstein', Floris Books, 2004, UK.

12. Senner, Madis, 'An Altar Can Transform Your Garden' via Geomantica magazine no. 50, September 2011. See - www.motherearthprayers.org

13. Moore Alanna, 'Divining Earth Spirit', Python Press, 2004, Australia.

14. Moore, Alanna, 'Touchstones for Today', Python Press, 2013, Australia.

♀PYTHON ♀PRESS

Books on eco-sensitive and sustainable living,
dowsing and awareness of the spiritual dimensions
of life and planet
www.pythonpress.com
pythonpress@gmail.com

Books by Alanna Moore:

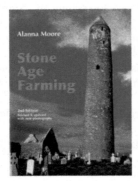

Stone Age Farming

**- tapping nature's energies
for your farm or garden**

From the mystery of Irish Round Towers to
modern Towers of Power for enhancing plant
growth. Exploring the energies of rocks and
landscapes from ancient folklore to modern
understandings, this book goes on to look at
practical applications in the garden, the
harnessing of our 'psychic' awareness with the art of dowsing and some
of its history. Eleven years after the 1st edition, Alanna has updated and
revised the book, describing the outcomes of installing Power Towers in
farms and gardens around Australasia.

Sensitive Permaculture

- cultivating the way of the sacred Earth
This book explores the living energies of the
land and how to sensitively connect with them.
Positively joyful, it draws on indigenous wisdom
of Australasia, Ireland and elsewhere, combining
the insights of geomancy and geobiology with
eco-smart permaculture design to offer an excit-
ing new paradigm for sustainable living.

What has been said about this book:
"A very practical and thoughtful guide for the eco-spiritual gardener, bringing awareness to the invisible dimensions of our landscape"
Rainbow News, New Zealand.

"An adventure in magical and practical Earth awareness"
Nexus magazine, Australia and global.

Water Spirits of the World

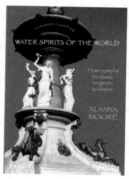

- from nymphs to nixies, serpents to sirens

This book delves into the esoteric aspects of water and the great variety of its other-dimensional denizens, including tales of real encounters with water beings.

What readers have said of the original edition of this book:
"A comprehensive collection of information and a rich insight into the world of water spirits ... including some wonderful stories of encounters with water spirits ... well researched and informative"
Martha Heeren, Dowser's Society NSW newsletter, April 2009.
"A wonderful resource book" Morgana, Wiccan Rede, Lammas 2009
This *"joyful travelogue of water spirits around the world has been a journey inspired by love"*   Anne Guest, Gatekeeper no. 26, UK.

Divining Earth Spirit
- an exploration of global
& Australasian Geomancy

From English ley lines and fairy folk, to geopathic stress and geo-mythos of the Aboriginal Dreamtime. This books explores the fact that the environment is alive and conscious!

"A classic for anyone wanting to get involved

with Earth healing. It contains information by the bucketload... The research that has gone into this book is incredible and no doubt will stir you into wanting to use it yourself"
Radionics Network, Vol. 2 No.6, Australia.

Touchstones for Today
- Designing for Earth harmony
with stone arrangements

From Britain's Stonehenge and stone altars in Ireland, to Aboriginal people's stone arrangements with cosmological connections in Australia, to modern labyrinth making - the urge to work with stones spans the world.

Be inspired to discover for yourself the magical energies associated with both ancient megalithic sites and modern stones of power. Find out how to create your own energetic stone arrangements for Earth harmony and ritual working with the sacred landscape.

Praise for this book:

"This book is a little goldmine of useful information... [it is] an easily accessible, concentrated repository of information on all things petrous." Grahame Gardner, President - British Society of Dowsers

"To Moore, these touchstones around the world are linked to a rich heritage that belongs to all of humanity. Her deep reverence for our sacred Earth is inspiring." Ruth Parnell, Nexus magazine, June/July 2013.

Geomantica

Resources for sensitive living and land caring
at www.geomantica.com

Courses and resources, books, DVDs, stone pendulums
and map dowsing service.

Diploma of Dowsing for Harmony

This correspondence course covers techniques and applications of pendulum dowsing that focus on creating a more energetically harmonious world. It can potentially lead the student towards a career, doing this work professionally. Many hundreds of students from around the world have enjoyed the opportunity for distant study. Originally written by Alanna Moore in 1989, it has been revised and updated over the years. The course can now be bought separately in ten parts, or all at once at a discounted price.

The course includes comprehensive notes, dowsing charts and lists, practical exercises, and interaction with course originator and internationally acclaimed tutor Alanna Moore, who has over 30 years experience in professional dowsing and the teaching of it.

You can start now or anytime and complete it in your own time, although generally it is usually undertaken over one or two years. There's no obligation when to finish.

This course has also now been made available to a wider audience, for people who don't want to achieve a Diploma, at a reduced fee.

See - **www.geomantica.com/dowsing-correspondence-course**

Map Dowsing Service

Do you sleep in a healthy place
and wake up feeling good and refreshed?
If not, would you like to find out if geopathic stress is affecting you?

Do you want to know where to put a Power Tower in
to make the garden grow better?
Or where to best locate a stone circle, at a strong energy centre?
Do you want to find out where the local nature spirits reside?

Find out such things and more, with a geomantic dowsing survey by
Alanna Moore. To identify areas of noxious or beneficial energies etc,
house and land surveys are available by remote map dowsing.

Hand drawn house plans are sufficient. Mark in the north point, street
address and any significant features at the site and email it across.
Affordable rates that must be pre-paid at the website.

For more information see
http://www.geomantica.com/services/map-dowsing/

Other Resources

German language:
Alanna Moore's 'Stone Age Farming' auf Deutsch: - from
http://mobiwell.com/stone-age-farming

Essbare Garten, Zhor Wust, **www.essbaregaerten.net**
also **www.agnikultur.de**, email - info@agnikultur.de

www.sprichmitdeinernahrung.blogspot.com ('speak to your food')

Chinese language:
Alanna Moore's 'Stone Age Farming' in Chinese - from
http://www.lapislazuli.org/tw/index.php

Lightning Source UK Ltd.
Milton Keynes UK
UKOW06f0407081117
312342UK00009B/165/P